SOVIET LEADERS

FROM LENIN TO GORBACHEV

SOVIET LEADERS

FROM LENIN TO GORBACHEV

Thomas Streissguth

Foreword by Alexander M. Haig, Jr.

illustrated with photographs

The Oliver Press, Inc.
Minneapolis

The Oliver Press
Josiah King House
2709 Lyndale Avenue South
Minneapolis, MN 55408

Library of Congress Cataloging-in-Publication Data

Streissguth, Thomas, 1958-
Soviet leaders from Lenin to Gorbachev / Thomas Streissguth :
foreword by Alexander M. Haig, Jr.

p. cm. — (Profiles)
Includes bibliographical references and index.
    Summary: Surveys the history of the Soviet Union through
the exploits and achievements of the seven men who were its leaders from 1917 to 1991; Vladimir Lenin, Joseph Stalin, Nikita
Khrushchev, Leonid Brezhnev, Yuri Andropov, Konstantin
Chernenko, and Mikhail Gorbachev.
ISBN 1-881508-02-1 : $14.95
1. Soviet Union—History—1917-   —Juvenile literature.
2. Heads of states—Soviet Union—Biography—Juvenile literature.
3. Communists—Soviet Union—Biography—Juvenile literature.
[1. Soviet Union—History. 2. Heads of state.] I. Title.
II. Series: Profiles (Minneapolis, Minn.)
DK253.S78   1992   92-19903
947.084'1—dc20   CIP
                                                            AC

ISBN 1-881508-02-1
Profiles I
Printed in the United States of America

99 98 97 96 95 94 93 92   8 7 6 5 4 3 2 1

Contents

Foreword 7

Introduction 9

Chapter 1 Vladimir Lenin..19

Chapter 2 Josef Stalin...45

Chapter 3 Nikita Khrushchev 69

Chapter 4 Leonid Brezhnev 93

Chapter 5 Yuri Andropov and
           Konstantin Chernenko 113

Chapter 6 Mikhail Gorbachev 127

Bibliography 154

Index 155

Russian revolutionaries used the ideas of Karl Marx, who lived from 1818 to 1883, to support the radical changes they made in their country.

Foreword

The sudden collapse of Soviet power must be ranked as the greatest, and least expected, event of our times. No one can say for certain when the peoples of this multinational empire lost their fear and brought it down. But down they pulled it amidst compelling evidence that it had failed to provide either bread or freedom.

This book tells the story of the leaders of one of the world's most powerful totalitarian dictatorships. The gallery of portaits shows that the Soviet Union was ruled by highly intelligent men, but men also capable of great cruelty. They all shared four flaws:

1) they were unaccountable to anyone except their own limited consciences, certainly not to the people;

2) the ideology they preached, like a religious cult, admitted of no errors, unlike a constitution that can be amended;

3) they did not respect individual rights, but instead saw people as cogs in the great machine of Marxism-Leninism that would bring all of humanity to paradise;

4) they saw most human values, such as telling the truth, as simply "optional," depending on whether it served the policy line of the moment.

As future generations assess the past, it may seem strange to them that such men could have ruled such a bad system for so long. Yet it happened in the absence of laws, a constitution, respect for individual rights and for simple decency. I hope that the lives of these Soviet leaders may instruct future generations on how *not* to conduct government. I also hope that this book will bring each reader a greater appreciation for America's constitutional democracy which depends so importantly on the sense of responsibility on the part of its citizens.

General Alexander M. Haig, Jr. (USA-Ret)
Former U. S. Secretary of State; NATO Commander;
White House Chief of Staff

Introduction

*O*n a cold December evening in 1991, the flag of the Soviet Union was lowered from its staff in the capital of Moscow. Within a few minutes, the white, blue, and red flag of the Russian republic rose in its place. The last Soviet leader had announced his resignation on national television, and the Soviet parliament would soon vote itself out of existence. In this way, one of the largest and most powerful empires in history quietly came to an end.

For 74 years, the leaders of the Soviet Union had ruled their country in the name of an idea—socialism. Karl Marx, a nineteenth-century German historian, had described this idea in his books. Marx wrote that, just as the night naturally follows the day, socialism would naturally follow capitalism. In capitalist nations, such as the United States and Canada, private individuals and corporations own the land and businesses, which they try to run for a profit. However, according to Marx, the government of a socialist nation would own all land, all factories, all banks, and shops. Workers and farmers would earn roughly equal wages. The government would plan the economy and provide for its citizens. This government would gradually shrink as society evolved toward a state of perfect equality known as communism.

Writing in the nineteenth century, Marx predicted that a revolution of industrial workers would someday bring about his socialist state. The twentieth century proved him right. In 1917, the revolution he foresaw occurred in the Russian Empire. A small group of Marxists led by Vladimir Lenin succeeded in overthrowing the Russian government. Marxists viewed this government, under the rule of the *tsar*, as oppressive, dictatorial, and privileged. To change their country from this rule by a few, Lenin and his followers confiscated private property and took complete control of the Russian economy. The new government under Lenin set up workers' councils called *soviets* to run factories and local governments. A union of several republics, led by these various councils and committees, replaced the Russian Empire. Thus, the Soviet Union was born.

Lenin was the first politician actually to build a socialist state. Through hard work and determination,

Vladimir Ilyich Lenin, founder of the Soviet Union

he tried to shape the Soviet Union into the communist image envisioned by Karl Marx. In order to accomplish this, Lenin fought a long and bloody civil war, and eliminated—by imprisonment, exile, or execution—those who opposed him. When Lenin died in 1924, the Communist party of the Soviet Union was the only legal political party in the USSR (Union of Soviet Socialist Republics).

However, although Lenin accomplished many things, he failed to create a fair and legal system of

11

electing new Soviet leaders. After Lenin's death, the highest officials of the Communist party battled each other to become the general secretary of the Communist party. This position was the country's most powerful job. A huge policy-making group arose under the general secretary to administer the country. Members of this bureaucracy did not run for office or win elections. Instead, they were simply appointed by their superiors, who measured their worth not by ability but by loyalty. Because of this system, the Russian socialist revolution created a new aristocracy that took the place of the privileged class that had ruled Russia before the revolution.

Lenin's successor, Josef Stalin, became the second Soviet leader by throwing his rivals out of the Communist party. Stalin then used the Party bureaucracy to impose a harsh dictatorship on the Soviet Union. Like the tsars of the old Russian Empire, he became an absolute ruler whose words and actions could not be questioned. Under Stalin, the government forgot the ideals of socialism—in which leaders would cooperate with their colleagues and with the people in leading the country. Instead, Stalin ruled both Party members and ordinary Soviet citizens through fear.

Stalin ruled during the most violent and difficult period of Soviet history. With brute force, he transformed the Soviet Union from a backward and poor agricultural nation into one of the world's mightiest industrial powers. In fact, Stalin's industrialization enabled his country to fight and win a devastating war with Germany in the early 1940s. As many as 20 million Soviet citizens were killed in this war.

Stalin bent the Communist party to his will and created a socialist dictatorship. During his years as general secretary, no one dared to question the leader, the Party, or the Soviet government. Party members never criticized "Stalinism," and workers lost their independence. Because the state took care of all economic planning and social needs, individual ambition and innovation ended.

Like Lenin, Stalin prepared no one to be his successor. In the late 1950s—several years after Stalin's death—Nikita Khrushchev became general secretary. Khrushchev condemned the Stalinist system and began a series of political and economic reforms in the Soviet Union.

By Khrushchev's time, however, the Communist party bureaucracy "owned" the Soviet Union. Communist officials controlled the production, distribution, and sale of all food, machinery, and consumer goods. In return for their loyal and unquestioning service, Party members won secure jobs and privileges denied to ordinary Soviet citizens.

Instead of the socialist, classless society predicted by Marx, the Soviet Union had become a nation of two distinct classes: those who joined the Party and rose to higher and higher positions of power, and the great majority of Soviet citizens who did not join the Party. Khrushchev's proposed reforms threatened the privileged Communist officials—some of whom were his rivals for power. In the early 1960s, several of his colleagues forced Khrushchev out of office.

Khrushchev's successor, Leonid Brezhnev, was a man of no particular talent or imagination. He became a Communist figurehead who simply gave speeches or made appearances. The Soviet bureaucracy took on a life of its own, rewarding its Party members and ignoring all others. The highest members of the Soviet government expressed a single opinion, always voting together on Soviet policy. The violence and fear of Stalin's reign were past, but the leaders still silenced or sent into exile those who questioned the Party's role in guiding the Soviet Union.

Brezhnev ruled at a time of increased Soviet influence abroad. As many countries in Africa and Asia gained independence, they tried the socialist system. Yet, by the 1980s the Soviet Union itself was stagnating. Central planning could not maintain this huge nation of far-flung cities and republics. Without competition, state-owned industries did not need to modernize. Factory production fell. Food shortages occurred. The living standards of ordinary Soviet citizens also fell—slowly at first, and then rapidly. Meanwhile, the elderly members of Brezhnev's government resisted change. At his death in 1982, the Soviet Union was running adrift like a great ship that had lost its rudder—and most of its power.

After the short terms of Yuri Andropov and Konstantin Chernenko, during which little changed, a new Soviet ruler came to power in March 1985. Mikhail Gorbachev, through ambition, energy, and loyalty, had risen quickly within the Party ranks. He had new ideas on how to run the Soviet economy and how to bring some prosperity back to his country. Gorbachev was convinced that his reforms could make Marx's socialism work. But as the years went by, and Gorbachev saw no improvement, he grew increasingly frustrated with the Party bureaucracy. Finally, in 1988, he transformed the leadership of the Soviet Union. He set up a system in which the people of the Soviet Union voted for a new Congress of People's Deputies. In this system, both Communists and non-Communists would compete in an open campaign for seats in the new legislature. The congress would, in turn, select an executive president. Under Gorbachev's plan, the Soviet president could serve two terms of five years. With one dramatic step, Gorbachev introduced a new concept into Soviet government—democracy.

Democracy, however, did not bring popularity to Gorbachev. By the late 1980s, food shortages were making many Soviet citizens angry. The economic reforms set in motion by Gorbachev were failing. In

Demonstrators rally in Cathedral Square, in Vilnius, Lithuania, to demand independence from the Soviet Union.

addition, many Soviet republics were demanding their independence from the USSR. The future looked bleak.

When conservative Soviet generals attempted to oust Gorbachev in August 1991, the people took to the streets to stop them. But this new revolution brought an end to the Communist party. Many of the 15 republics of the Soviet Union voted to go their own way as independent nations. Gorbachev could do nothing to stop them. Gradually the Soviet Union disintegrated. In

December 1991, Gorbachev resigned as the Soviet president. On the same day, Russian guards changed the flags flying over Moscow. Gorbachev, who wanted to modernize and revive the Soviet system, instead became the last Soviet leader. The state Lenin had founded proved unable to provide its promised socialist future to the people of the USSR. Instead, socialism in Russia proved as harsh and oppressive as the rule of the Russian tsars. In the end, like tsardom, it bowed to the people's will.

Lenin and his wife, Nadezhda Krupskaya, in 1919. The couple met in underground Marxist circles in St. Petersburg, and married in Siberia in 1898.

1
Vladimir Lenin

Russia in the nineteenth century was a state without a parliament, without elections, and without political parties. This vast empire was ruled by a tsar—an absolute monarch whose word was law. Most of the tsar's subjects were poor laborers who lived on farming estates and in country villages. Many of these peasants were serfs. They were not allowed to leave the estates on which they lived and worked. Moreover, they were the private property of the landowners. In 1861 Tsar Alexander II granted the serfs their freedom. But their lives did not improve. Many owed large sums of money to the landowners for their freedom. Disease and hunger were widespread, and most peasants could raise barely

Tsar Alexander II, who tried to reform Russia gradually, was killed by a bomb-throwing terrorist in 1881.

enough food on their small plots of land to feed their families.

In Russian cities, factories were just beginning to employ large numbers of industrial workers. Conditions for working people in the cities were poor. Hours were long; the work was dirty and dangerous; and the pay was barely enough for survival. The tsars, who took no action to improve the lives of their subjects, were deeply suspicious of anyone demanding reform.

In the middle of this empire, in Simbirsk on the banks of the Volga River in central Russia, Vladimir Ilyich Ulyanov (or Lenin) was born in 1870. After leaving Simbirsk, Vladimir Lenin would embark on a journey that would change this empire—and with it, the world.

Lenin, who brought down the Russian Empire in the name of the workers and the peasants, never labored in a factory or a field. His family owned houses and property in Simbirsk, and in the nearby countryside. Lenin's father, Ilya Ulyanov, was a school director. His mother, Maria, came from the Russian capital of St. Petersburg and was the daughter of a German doctor. As a school official, Ilya Ulyanov belonged to the nobility and was loyal to the tsar and to the Russian government.

Vladimir Lenin was the third of six children. He was close to his older brother, Alexander, who attended a university in St. Petersburg in the 1880s. At this school, Alexander Ulyanov joined a group of students who sought to change social conditions within Russia. But because the Russian people could not pass laws or demand reforms, the students could do little but talk.

To find a way to bring change to their country, the students read the works of European writers and philosophers. One of these writers, Karl Marx, was a German who had spent much of his life in England. Marx believed that dissatisfied workers would eventually rise up and overthrow their governments. They would then put in place socialism—a new system in which workers would own land, factories, and machinery in

Lenin's parents, Ilya Nikolayevich Ulyanov and Maria Alexandrovna Ulyanov

The Ulyanov family in 1879. Standing from left, the children are Olga, Alexander, and Anna. Seated are baby Maria, Dimitri, and Vladimir.

22

common. Marx believed that when socialism finally succeeded in providing a fair share to everyone, government itself would gradually disappear. People would enjoy both equality and prosperity.

Marx had a loyal following in nineteenth-century Russia. Socialist groups in St. Petersburg formed to read and discuss Marxist writings, and to recruit factory workers to their cause. However, these groups saw little hope of Marx's industrial revolution for factory workers taking place in Russia because most Russians still lived and worked in the countryside as peasants.

Many socialists came up with a simple solution to their dilemma: they would assassinate the tsar. By killing the Russian leader, they believed, they could bring about change immediately.

Alexander Ulyanov, Lenin's older brother, joined one of these revolutionary groups in St. Petersburg. In March 1887, Alexander's group attempted to kill the tsar by throwing a bomb at his carriage. They failed, and the police arrested Alexander and several others. In May 1887, the Russian government put Alexander to death for taking part in the plot against the tsar.

The death of his brother overwhelmed Vladimir Lenin, who at the time was preparing for a university career. Although Lenin entered the University of Kazan that fall, he was under suspicion as the brother of a convicted assassin. Within a few months, the university expelled Lenin for taking part in a noisy student meeting.

Lenin managed, however, to continue his studies, although for several years the government did not allow him to enroll in another school. Eventually the University of St. Petersburg accepted him as a student—but did not allow him to attend classes. While studying at home, he mastered a course in law. In just over a year, he passed the university's law examination at the top of his class.

After graduating, Lenin joined a small law firm in the town of Samara. But he had few clients and attended few trials. Instead, he devoted most of his time to the study of Marx and other writers who had guided his brother, Alexander. One of these was Nikolai Chernyshevsky, a Russian author who had written a novel called *What Is to Be Done?* This book changed Lenin's life.

In his novel, Chernyshevsky insisted that individuals, no matter what their beliefs, must be wholly dedicated to their goals. The writer expressed contempt for people who would compromise their principles by agreeing with their enemies. Chernyshevsky was talking about the small group of Russian political "liberals" who sought to form an elected Russian parliament and to work within a democratic system to bring about reform.

Lenin read Chernyshevsky's novel several times, trying to learn its lessons. Badly written and not very popular, *What Is to Be Done?* inspired Lenin's dedication to a Russian revolution. Like the characters in the novel, he

A typical St. Petersburg street in the early 1900s

would never negotiate with his enemies—which included the tsar, the liberals, the landowners, and the social class into which he had been born.

In 1893, Lenin left central Russia for the capital of St. Petersburg, where the country's largest mass of factory workers lived. Lenin joined Marxist circles that met in secret to discuss revolutionary books and articles. At one meeting, Lenin met Nadezhda Krupskaya, who later became his wife.

In 1895 Lenin traveled to Switzerland to meet Georgy Plekhanov, a famous Russian Marxist who was living in exile. Lenin's dedication to socialism impressed Plekhanov. However, while he favored cooperating with the Russian liberals, Lenin rejected this view.

In a few years, this disagreement would break the Russian socialist party in half.

After a wave of strikes broke out among Russian workers in the fall of 1895, Lenin returned to St. Petersburg. Upon arriving in the capital, he took charge of the socialists who were organizing the strikers. The police, who considered Lenin dangerous, followed him closely and planted a spy within his group. In December, they arrested Lenin. After spending a year in jail, he was sent to Siberia, a remote region of Russia where he would be unlikely to cause any trouble. The police allowed Krupskaya, who was also arrested, to travel east with Lenin on condition the two would be married.

In 1898, while Lenin was marking time in a small Siberian village, the socialists founded the Social Democratic (SD) party. Despite this new name, the socialist movement was not united. Some socialists called for a new Russian democracy, with regular elections and a representative parliament. Others, like Lenin, wanted to establish a "dictatorship of the proletariat"—a government run solely by representatives of the factory workers.

Lenin's exile ended in 1900. Knowing that the tsar's police would be watching him, he again left Russia and traveled to Switzerland. This time, he had a project in mind. While in Siberia, he had planned a new socialist newspaper that would be printed abroad and then distributed to the Russian workers. The paper would provide a detailed plan for the future Russian revolution.

The first edition of this paper—*Iskra* (meaning "The Spark")—was printed in Germany on a printing press that was kept secret. Smugglers brought copies of *Iskra*

The first issue of Iskra *was printed in December 1900. Its editorial board consisted of V.I. Lenin, G.V. Plekhanov (top), Y.O. Martov, V.I. Zasulich, P.B. Akselrod, and A.P. Potresov (center, from left). N.K. Krupskaya (bottom) served as secretary.*

across the Russian border and then to the cities. There the socialists read it aloud at secret meetings and distributed it on the street. Lenin wrote many of the paper's articles. In his articles, Lenin called for a new party of professional, full-time revolutionaries who would educate the factory workers and direct the overthrow of the Russian government.

Although socialism was gaining favor among Russian workers, conflict was brewing within the SD party. At a meeting in 1903, Lenin argued with the other socialists over the party's organization. Lenin wanted to form a small group of paid, professional revolutionaries who would follow the directions of a central committee. According to Lenin's plan, the workers would have no say in party organization or tactics. Lenin played a trick on his rivals by having his smaller group called the *Bolsheviks*—from the Russian word for "majority."

Socialists opposed to this "Leninism" formed a group that became known as *Mensheviks* ("minority"). The Mensheviks favored open party membership and an elected Russian parliament. They wanted to form labor unions among the workers. These unions would insist, in a legal and orderly way, that factory owners initiate changes. The two socialist groups—the Bolsheviks and the Mensheviks—could not smooth out their differences, and instead became bitter rivals.

In 1905, when the Russian Empire suffered a crushing military defeat at the hands of Japan, both socialist groups saw an opportunity for revolution. By losing thousands of men and much of its navy, the tsar's government became the object of scorn and ridicule among the Russian people. Soldiers and sailors mutinied, and rioting took place in St. Petersburg and Moscow. The tsar's loyal Cossack guards crushed the demonstrations, but the fires of revolution had been lit.

Leon Trotsky, a friend of Lenin's who had joined the Mensheviks in 1903, formed a council of workers and soldiers, known as a soviet, in St. Petersburg. Later, soviets, or councils, would form in Moscow and in other large Russian cities. The soviets planned and coordinated strikes and protests by the workers. Most members of Trotsky's St. Petersburg soviet were Mensheviks.

Fearing more violence, Tsar Nicholas II allowed Russian politicians to form a parliament known as the *Duma*. This body could only advise the tsar on political matters, however. It had no power to pass legislation. In a gesture of goodwill, Nicholas granted a general pardon to all political prisoners and exiles. Because of this, Lenin returned to Russia in the fall of 1905.

Lenin quickly saw that the Duma, by allowing public debate, was taking some of the steam out of the revolution. Demonstrations and strikes were becoming rare, and the tsar's government seemed ready to grant some reforms. Even worse, to Lenin's way of thinking, the Bolsheviks reconciled with the Mensheviks in 1906. Lenin refused to be a part of this compromise, and formed his own small Bolshevik faction, or clique. When the police issued a warrant for his arrest in 1907, he again fled the country.

Lenin began to organize Russian socialists abroad. Moving from city to city, he attended meetings and wrote pamphlets. But as the months and years went by, Lenin lost touch with many of his followers at home and began losing support among the Russian workers. Tsar Nicholas and his aides allowed some reforms, and the lives of many peasants and factory workers were improving. The industrialization of Russian cities was creating a growing middle class that supported democracy—not revolution.

With little money coming in from his writing, Lenin accepted criminal actions to support his Bolshevik party. His comrades within Russia, including Josef Stalin, organized robberies of banks and stagecoaches. The Bolsheviks even tried to counterfeit Russian money. Through these and other means, the Bolsheviks gradually improved their finances. In addition, Lenin's editorials in the new socialist newspaper *Pravda* ("Truth") kept his blueprint for revolution before the public eye. Lenin was certain that, just as Marx had predicted, the workers would eventually revolt against their governments. But he could do little organizing while living far from Russia in the Swiss city of Zurich.

By 1914, Russia and the European nations were preparing for war. Germany and Great Britain were

Russian soldiers in a World War I trench

building up their armed forces and forming alliances with other European nations. In August 1914, fighting broke out along Russia's border with Germany. Incompetent generals led the Russian troops, and the army lacked food, ammunition, and arms. In a series of bloody battles, the German troops inflicted terrible defeats on the Russian army.

Many socialists, and most of the Russian people, supported the war, but Lenin was opposed to Russia's conflict with Germany. He feared that the war would raise popular support for the tsar and the Russian government. Through his writing, Lenin urged Russian soldiers to stop fighting and to return to their homes.

By 1916, as Lenin had hoped, support for the war was falling. The situation on the battlefield was disastrous.

Tsar Nicholas moved to the war front to oversee the campaign personally. His wife, the Empress Alexandra, remained in the capital. With the advice of incapable aides, she canceled all the reforms allowed by the government before the war. The government ignored demands for peace. In the Russian cities, shortages of food caused long lines, high prices, and angry remarks.

By March 1917, the situation grew violent. A shortage of bread in St. Petersburg—which had been renamed Petrograd—caused a sudden strike of workers. The work in factories came to a stop as unruly mobs swept through the city's streets. Tsar Nicholas called on the army regiments near the city to put down the strike and to force the workers back to their jobs. But instead of confronting the demonstrators, the soldiers simply stood their ground and refused to fire.

The government had completely lost control of its capital. Members of the Duma met the tsar while he was returning to the capital on his personal train. Nicholas, realizing that his authority had disappeared, agreed to give up his throne.

Russian politicians set up a new provisional, or temporary, government in the capital. The Petrograd soviet allowed many members of the competing socialist factions—including Bolsheviks—to join their council. The provisional government granted freedom to Russian political prisoners. Once again, Lenin saw his opportunity, but he could not return to Russia. European

Tsar Nicholas II, the last member of the Romanov family to rule Russia (from 1894 to 1917), was executed, along with his family, by Bolshevik revolutionaries in July 1918.

nations that wanted to keep this dangerous revolutionary safely in Switzerland denied him permission to cross their territory. A thousand miles from home, Lenin could only sit and watch, while the revolution he had been planning for years took place without him.

Although the tsar had fallen, most Russian soldiers stayed at the front where the fighting with Germany was taking place. Germany's leaders, who were fighting the forces of several nations to the west and east, saw a way to end their war with Russia: they would help the workers continue the Russian revolution. Thus the provisional Russian government would become involved in putting down the revolution and would be unable to continue fighting the war. To make this come about, German leaders allowed Lenin to cross German territory in a sealed train. After passing through Germany, Sweden, and Finland, Lenin's train arrived in Petrograd on April 16, 1917.

A huge crowd greeted Lenin at the capital's Finland Station. Lenin stepped onto the platform and announced his plans to a cheering crowd. The abdication of the tsar was only the first stage, he declared. The workers must now demand "all power to the soviets" and prepare to overthrow the provisional government.

For the Mensheviks, however, the revolution was over—it was time to elect a constituent assembly, which would write a new Russian constitution. Moreover, many Bolsheviks favored working within the provisional government. Lenin would not compromise, however. But his party, a faction of the Bolshevik party, was still quite small—only a few thousand full-time members— and Mensheviks led most of the soviets, or councils.

Lenin felt that, in this time of chaos and uncertainty, his small and determined organization had the advantage. During the next few months, while politicians battled in the provisional government and accomplished little, Lenin and the Bolsheviks who followed him repeated a simple promise to the Russian people— "Land, Bread, and Peace."

In July 1917, violent demonstrations broke out

against the provisional government in Petrograd. This time the Bolsheviks took an active role in the rioting. Alexander Kerensky, the leader of the government, ordered Lenin's arrest. Kerensky ordered the publication of forged papers that seemed to prove that Lenin was in the pay of the German government. Disguised as a worker, Lenin escaped at the last minute across the border to Finland.

From his hiding place, Lenin realized that the time for a Bolshevik revolt was fast approaching. The situation at the war front was chaotic: peasant soldiers were deserting their units, returning home, and seizing

Alexander Kerensky (1881-1970), prime minister of the provisional government, kept Russia in the war while Lenin promised peace.

estates from Russian landowners. In the cities, food shortages worsened. Government troops were firing on demonstrators. The violent response of the provisional government in July had turned many of the city's workers against Kerensky. The Bolsheviks, who were still a small minority in the Duma, began to gain popular support. They also managed to take control of the Petrograd soviet.

In September, Lvar Georgyevich Kornilov, a general for the tsar, prepared an attack on the capital to overthrow the provisional government. Desperate, Kerensky released hundreds of Bolsheviks from prison and armed them. Kornilov's attack failed. But under the direction of Leon Trotsky, who had joined the Bolsheviks, the revolutionaries organized themselves into a disciplined fighting force known as the Red Guards.

From his hiding place in Finland, Lenin worked hard to bring new members into the Bolshevik party. He wrote articles and pamphlets denouncing Kerensky. He urged his Bolshevik comrades to seize the government ministries. In the fall of 1917, Lenin declared, "Now or never!"

On October 25, Lenin slipped across the border and returned to Petrograd. At a Bolshevik meeting, he convinced party members that the time for open revolt had come. Trotsky's Red Guards occupied bridges, telegraph stations, train stations, and major intersections in Petrograd. On the next day, a small force attacked and

Leon Trotsky as a
young man

People's Commissar for Military and Naval Affairs Leon
Trotsky (in overcoat) leads a military parade of Red Guards
in Moscow's Red Square.

occupied the Winter Palace, where the provisional government met. As Kerensky and other government ministers fled the city, the Bolsheviks declared that the soviets now ruled Petrograd. Within days, the Bolsheviks established a new Council of People's Commissars, with Lenin as its head.

Having won Petrograd, Lenin now had to extend the Bolsheviks' control to the rest of the country. Soviets in Russian towns and factories seized power in the name of the workers. To win over the Russian peasants to the revolution, the Bolsheviks abolished all private land ownership. They broke up the huge estates on which the Russian serfs had once labored, and turned the land over to committees of peasants.

The Winter Palace in Petrograd, seat of the provisional government

Red Guards outside the Smolny Institute in Petrograd, in October 1917

In December 1917, Lenin set up a secret police organization, the *Cheka*. During the next few years, the Cheka arrested and imprisoned millions of the Bolsheviks' enemies. In January 1918, the constituent assembly promised by the provisional government met for the first and last time. This group was supposed to write a new Russian constitution. Lenin ordered the Red Guards to close down the assembly at gunpoint.

The new Soviet government was still at war with Germany. Although many Bolsheviks wanted to continue the fighting, Lenin argued for peace at any cost. He knew that a German victory in western Russia would end the Bolshevik revolution. German armies would overthrow the Soviet government in Petrograd, arrest Lenin and execute him.

After taking a vote in the Central Committee, the Soviet government agreed to the Treaty of Brest-Litovsk in March 1918. Because of this treaty, large territories were lost to Germany or became independent. However, German forces continued to occupy the Ukraine, a large region in the western part of the old Russian Empire. To put some distance between his government and the German forces, Lenin moved his government from Petrograd to Moscow.

Despite the peace, Lenin's troubles were not over. The revolt of 1917 had hurt millions of peasants, landowners, and government workers. Food supplies were still scarce, and Russian factories remained idle. Opponents of the Bolshevik government rallied large forces of troops and officers still loyal to Tsar Nicholas II. Lenin's government in Moscow controlled only those cities that had loyal Bolshevik soviets. In the rest of the country chaos reigned.

The Bolsheviks needed to keep the large Russian cities loyal to their revolution. To ensure this loyalty, Lenin ordered that grain be taken by force from the peasants, and used to feed the unemployed workers in the cities. Soviets seized heavy equipment, arms, and raw materials from private firms. These policies, known as "war communism," turned much of the country against the Bolsheviks at a crucial time.

Despite the growing opposition, Lenin never turned away from his goal of setting up a one-party state.

Because of this, he still had many enemies among the Mensheviks and among other socialists who feared a Bolshevik dictatorship. Many of his opponents fled the country and went abroad; others joined counterrevolutionary armies or took more direct action. On August 30, a socialist named Fanny Kaplan shot Lenin twice as he was leaving a workers' meeting in Moscow. Although Lenin recovered, this attempt on his life made him more determined than ever to put a violent end to his opponents within Russia.

By the fall of 1918, the Bolsheviks, led by Lenin, were fighting a full-scale civil war. Troops and officers loyal to the tsar banded together and formed their own armies. Known as "Whites," the tsarist troops sought to overthrow the Bolshevik government by seizing the country's industrial centers. Soldiers from Britain and the United States landed in northern Russian ports to support the White armies. This civil war, which lasted three years, caused widespread destruction and starvation.

During this time, the Bolsheviks held on to the largest Russian cities, and in 1920 the tsarist White forces gradually disintegrated. Lenin and the Bolsheviks had won. But the civil war caused the total breakdown of agriculture and industry in Russia. Much of the countryside lay in ruins, and both peasants and city dwellers were dying of hunger and disease.

To bring about a recovery of the devastated Russian economy, Lenin created the New Economic Policy

A grisly civil war scene from Omsk, east of the Ural Mountains, where White army soldiers shot workers and peasants in 1919

(NEP) in 1921. The NEP eased government control over Russian businesses. It allowed small private shops, and factories were to compete with larger industries run by the state. Lenin considered the NEP a necessary—but temporary—step on the road to Russian socialism. Although many Bolsheviks opposed the NEP, others saw the policy as a way for the party to strengthen its hold on the country by improving the economy. In 1922, the Communist (formerly Bolshevik) party founded the Union of Soviet Socialist Republics (USSR)—a federation of republics that had once belonged to the Russian Empire, namely, Russia, Ukraine, and Byelorussia, as well as a group of territories to the south known as the Transcaucasian Federation.

By the early 1920s, Lenin was in ill health. In 1922 a stroke left him partially paralyzed. In the next year, another stroke confined him to his house, unable to speak. From his home, Lenin began to realize that instead of ridding his country of a corrupt government bureaucracy, he had simply created a new one.

To streamline the Bolshevik government, Lenin appointed Josef Stalin as "general secretary" in March 1922. Within a few months, Stalin was using his job to throw his rivals out of the Communist party and to gain as much personal control of the Party as possible.

To stop the quarreling, Lenin proposed to reorganize the government bureaus and work Stalin out of his post. But Lenin was too ill to attend party meetings. Without his presence, his plans were not carried out. Through violence and threats, Stalin steadily gained control of the party, and Lenin could do little to stop him.

Instead, in 1923, Lenin proposed a series of new laws that legalized arrest and execution for political crimes, including the crime of plotting against the state. Under the future dictatorship of Josef Stalin, these laws would send millions of Russians to their deaths at the hands of the Soviet secret police and the Soviet court system.

Lenin suffered another stroke in January 1924 and died on January 21. After his death, the Soviet leaders and the Russian people revered him as the guiding hand of the Bolshevik party and the creator of the modern

Soviet state. Instead of an ordinary grave, the Soviet leaders prepared an elaborate mausoleum in Moscow, in which Lenin's body is still preserved and on display.

Lenin remains the leading figure of the Russian revolution, which he shaped through a strong will, a creative imagination, and hard work. But the socialist state that he founded never lived up to Marx's goal of a classless and prosperous society. As a result, Lenin himself has lost his standing among people in the former Soviet Union and among people around the world who lived and worked within socialist states. His revolution will forever remain unfinished.

On a cold winter day in 1925, thousands of Soviets visit Lenin's tomb.

2
Josef Stalin

*M*any Russian Marxists were educated people who came from prosperous homes. Few revolutionaries, in fact, were members of the working class. Lenin, the founder of the Bolshevik party, once remarked that he was "the son of a squire."

Josef Stalin's childhood, however, was harsh and poor. His education was strict, and he spent much of his youth in prisons or in Siberian exile. These experiences shaped Stalin into a merciless leader who punished an entire nation through fear and dictatorship.

Stalin was born as Iosif Vissarionovich Dzhugashvili on December 21, 1879, in the small town of Gori in Georgia, a remote region in the southern part of the

Russian Empire. His family had moved to Gori from the Georgian countryside, where his father, Vissarion Dzhugashvili, had labored as a serf. After gaining his freedom, Dzhugashvili became a cobbler. Stalin's mother, Katerina Geladze, worked as a washerwoman. Before Iosif Dzhugashvili was born, three of Katerina's children had died while still infants. She was devoted to her only living child, and worked hard to pay for his schooling.

Stalin's father, however, was a violent man. He had little affection for the boy and often beat him. Vissarion Dzhugashvili eventually left the family and moved into a rooming house, where he lived alone. When Iosif was 11 years old, Vissarion was killed in a drunken brawl. By the time he was a teenager, Stalin had experienced poverty, pain, and fear. He had also learned to conquer his troubles by showing no emotion—and no pity.

Stalin attended a church school in Gori until he was 14 years old. He was a rebellious and stubborn young Georgian who hated the school's strict teachers, who were Russians. He fought with both teachers and fellow students and often suffered harsh punishments. Yet he was also a good student who, at the age of 17, graduated in the top rank of his class.

Despite his ability, Stalin's future was dim. The Russian authorities did not permit universities in Georgia, and the only way for a son of Georgian peasants to improve his life was to become a priest. By saving every penny she earned, Stalin's mother paid his tuition to a seminary in Tiflis (now Tbilisi), the capital of Georgia.

The priests at the Tiflis seminary, like the teachers at the school in Gori, were Russians, not Georgians. Their task was to train loyal members of the Church and to stamp out any rebellion against the tsar among the Georgian students. The seminarians followed a strict program of studies, and the priests allowed no argument in the classrooms. They punished students who criticized the tsar or the tsarist government or who read certain books. Once, for reading a banned novel by the French writer Victor Hugo, Stalin was banished to a solitary cell.

Stalin (center) with his Georgian friend, Avel Yenukidze, and Soviet writer Maxim Gorky (right)

Stalin, however, was a headstrong student whom the priests could not frighten. He defied the seminary's rules and read whatever he pleased. One of the banned writers whom Stalin favored was Karl Marx, who in his works predicted a worldwide revolution of factory workers against their bosses and governments. By the time Stalin was 18, he was leading an underground Marxist circle at the seminary. This group met late at night in secret to discuss the works of Marx and of other revolutionary writers. Stalin also joined the Social Democratic party in Tiflis and attended workers' meetings. There he recruited local factory workers to the Marxist cause.

The authorities expelled Stalin from the seminary in his fifth year for missing an examination. He then took a job as a clerk, but spent most of his time organizing the workers of Tiflis. By now the Social Democratic party had gained the close attention of the tsar's secret police, the *Okhrana*. In 1901 Okhrana agents raided the city of Tiflis and arrested all the revolutionaries they could find. Stalin managed to slip away, however, and went underground.

In November 1901, Stalin left Tiflis for Batum, a town on the nearby coast of the Black Sea. There he organized a strike among oil workers. After the police arrested many of the strikers, Stalin gathered several hundred local people for a march on the city's jail. As the marchers neared their destination, a line of policemen opened fire on the demonstrators. Stalin escaped the scene, but the police killed many marchers and bystanders.

Many Social Democrats throughout the Russian Empire were unhappy with Stalin's violent march in Batum. Not wanting any further battles with the police, they prepared to throw the young Georgian out of the party. Just before his expulsion, however, Stalin was arrested and jailed. In 1903, the authorities sent him into exile in distant Siberia.

Soon after Stalin's arrest, the Social Democrats split into two groups—the Mensheviks and the Bolsheviks. Although both factions were socialists, the Bolsheviks and their leader, Vladimir Lenin, sought to overthrow the Russian government and its ruler, the tsar, through a violent revolution. Moreover, the Bolsheviks would not share power with the Mensheviks or with any other revolutionary party. Stalin, like Lenin, approved of revolutionary violence and never compromised with his enemies. He also saw that his chances of rising to power were greater within the smaller ranks of the Bolshevik faction. For these reasons, he eventually sided with Lenin and the Bolsheviks.

Stalin spent 14 years of his life—from 1903 until 1917—in prison or in hiding. The tsarist government shipped him to tiny, poor Siberian villages, where he endured cold, hunger, and isolation. These years of imprisonment and exile made him bitter and suspicious.

Even after Stalin became a free man and a powerful leader, he trusted no one and showed no pity for his enemies.

Stalin managed to escape from prison five times. Each time, he returned to Georgia. There he planned bank robberies and other daring crimes that brought desperately needed money into the Bolshevik party. Some Bolsheviks opposed these actions. They felt that bank robbery was a bad way to support their revolution. Lenin, however, approved of these "expropriations," and Stalin paid no attention to the criticism. Lenin and Stalin accepted any methods that might bring Bolshevik rule—including robbery and murder. In the future, neither man would hesitate to use violence or treachery to gain his ends.

After the 1905 revolution broke out, the Socialists invited Stalin to a party conference in Tammerfors, Finland. There he heard Lenin speak of the future of Russia under Bolshevik rule. Lenin's intelligence and determination impressed Stalin. He decided to team up with Lenin, who had become the most powerful man in the party.

Lenin, for his part, was happy to have Josef Stalin join him in his efforts to change Russia through revolution. Lenin needed Stalin's ambition and toughness. But other Bolsheviks, many of whom were living in exile in foreign countries, scorned Stalin as an unsophisticated peasant.

Though from very different backgrounds, Lenin and Stalin gained much from each other politically. Within 18 months of this 1922 photo, Lenin would be dead and Stalin striving for complete control of the Soviet Union.

Many of these revolutionaries could argue for hours over the fine points in a book or a magazine article. But Stalin didn't enjoy fine conversation. He resented people who had a better education than he had or who were witty and smart. He had nothing but contempt for party members who lived safely abroad. Stalin scorned these members who talked and wrote in safety while real revolutionaries risked their lives and freedom within Russia.

Stalin had another valuable characteristic—his

nationality. The Bolsheviks, most of whom were Russians, needed to bring Georgians, Armenians, Balts, and other people from all parts of the vast Russian Empire over to their side. As a Georgian, Stalin could help the Bolsheviks recruit new members in the far corners of the empire.

In 1912 Lenin sent Stalin an assignment: he was to write an article on the future these minority groups would enjoy when they came under Bolshevik rule. The article appeared in *Pravda*, the party's newspaper. Under the article, and for the first time, Iosif Dzhugashvili signed his name "Stalin," meaning "man of steel." Stalin became known as an expert on the empire's minorities—despite the fact that many of his phrases and ideas were taken directly from Lenin's writings.

After four straight years of Siberian exile, Stalin was released in March 1917, after the overthrow of Tsar Nicholas II. He immediately boarded a train for Petrograd (the new name for St. Petersburg). While Lenin and other Bolshevik exiles remained in Zurich, Stalin settled in the capital and took control of *Pravda*.

After the fall of the tsar, a great debate raged among the Bolsheviks over whether they should cooperate with the new provisional, or temporary, government in Petrograd. Since the Bolsheviks still made up a small party with little influence over events, Stalin favored taking part in this provisional government. Lenin, however, argued with the Bolsheviks. He wanted to seize power by using a small group of armed revolutionaries to take control of city streets and government offices. After Lenin's opinions appeared in *Pravda* in April 1917, Stalin changed his opinion about the provisional government and supported revolution.

In the fall of 1917, as the provisional government weakened, the Bolshevik party saw its chance to take power. Lenin returned to Petrograd from Finland. Leon Trotsky, a friend of Lenin's, was organizing Bolshevik workers into armed Red Guard units. In late October, the Red Guard stormed the Winter Palace and overthrew the provisional government. Stalin, who had joined the Bolsheviks' Central Committee, stayed clear of the action that night. While the new Bolshevik state was being born, he was safe at a friend's apartment.

Russia spent the next three years in civil war, as followers of the tsar fought the Bolsheviks for control of Russia's major cities and industrial centers. Stalin became a messenger for Lenin and the Central Committee. He traveled to the war fronts, organized supplies, and rallied the Bolshevik soldiers.

After the Bolshevik victory in 1920, Stalin became the general secretary of the Central Committee. As head of the committee's *Secretariat*, he organized the Party and appointed its officials. Although he was not well known outside the Bolshevik (now Communist) party, Stalin used his position to increase his own power steadily. He eliminated his rivals by banishing them to insignificant jobs in distant cities. A personal network of spies helped him to keep a close watch on the Party's many bureaus and committees.

Lenin's health began to fail in late 1922. By then the Communist leader was having doubts about Stalin. He could see that Stalin wanted to bring the Party under his personal control. However, Lenin had neither the time nor the energy to get rid of the stubborn Georgian.

In his will, Lenin warned Party leaders that Stalin was not fit to lead the Communist party. Lenin claimed Stalin was simply "too rude in his personal relationships" to be effective. Suggesting that the Party should reorganize the Secretariat, Lenin also recommended that his colleagues find a way to remove Stalin.

As Lenin's health continued to decline, Stalin formed close ties with two other Communist leaders, Lev Kamenev and Grigory Zinoviev. These three formed an alliance against Trotsky, whom they saw as a threat. After Lenin suffered a stroke in 1923 that left him unable to speak, Stalin took on many of Lenin's responsibilities. But Lenin continued to write to Party officials to warn them against Stalin.

Before these officials could take action, however, Lenin died. The Party was now without its leader, and Stalin, Trotsky, Zinoviev, and Kamenev were guiding a huge country that was still in the process of rebuilding its economy and government.

Lenin's will nearly ruined Stalin. After the funeral,

Lenin's widow brought the document to be read before the entire Central Committee. Stalin sat, silent and embarrassed, as Lenin's harsh words rang out in the hall. But in his will, Lenin had also criticized other members of the *Politburo* (the highest ruling council), including Kamenev and Zinoviev.

Stalin saw this as a chance to save his job. After making an emotional speech, in which he openly admitted his faults, he offered to resign from the Politburo and from the Party. Zinoviev then came to Stalin's defense with a rousing speech, urging that the Party remain united. Zinoviev's support helped Stalin to gain re-election to his post as general secretary.

Lev Kamenev, perhaps Lenin's closest associate, joined Stalin and Grigory Zinoviev to lead the country after Lenin's death.

During the next five years, Stalin forced all his former supporters out of their posts. By joining first with one and then with another of his partners, he gained uncontested control of the Politburo. In late 1927, Leon Trotsky attempted to organize a public demonstration against Stalin. But many of the Russian people disliked Trotsky, who seemed to set himself above the country's everyday problems.

Trotsky's demonstration was a failure, and in 1927 Stalin convinced the Central Committee to expel him from the Party. Two years later Stalin forced Trotsky to leave the country. From abroad, he continued to criticize Stalin as a dictator who was betraying the ideas of Vladimir Lenin and the Bolsheviks.

By 1929 Stalin had become the most powerful individual in the Soviet government. His colleagues in the Politburo, who feared his large network of spies, no longer questioned his decisions or criticized his ideas. To help his own reputation, Stalin changed the official accounts of the revolution. In Stalin's new version of events, the revolution officially became the work of two men—Lenin and Stalin. Stalin then eliminated many of the old Bolsheviks who knew the truth about his minor role in the revolution. He even jailed, exiled, or had shot some of his own relatives who may have talked too much about his past.

As his power grew, Stalin began to suspect the presence of rivals and enemies everywhere. He became paranoid. Especially threatening to him were the Western countries, such as Great Britain, France, and the United States, that were far ahead of the Soviet Union in industrial production. Stalin, and many Soviet citizens, believed that these wealthier nations were planning to overthrow the Communist state. To meet this threat, Stalin began a massive program of industrialization in the late 1920s. He ordered Party officials to draw up a Five Year Plan that would quickly turn the Soviet Union into a modern industrial power.

The Five Year Plan reached into every corner of the Soviet economy. The largest disruption, however, occurred in the countryside. In order to build the new factories that would produce the steel, iron, heavy equipment, and electricity necessary for industrial power, the government needed more grain to feed workers in the cities. So, it seized all private farmland and set up huge, state-owned farms. The government forced millions of rural peasants onto these "collectives" and herded others into the cities to work in factories. The government then shipped all available grain to the cities, leaving little for rural people. To protest these governmental actions, the peasants burned their fields and slaughtered their animals. The result was a terrible famine in which millions in the Ukraine and central Russia starved.

Many wealthier peasants, or *kulaks*, who owned a few work animals or some outdated farming equipment, refused to take part in this "collectivization." Since the kulaks were responsible for much of the country's food production, Stalin had to overcome their resistance to his policies. To accomplish this, government officials set the poorer peasants against the kulaks by promising that the kulaks would have to give up their land to the collectives. The authorities rounded up and shot many kulaks. They exiled some to Siberia or to other remote and barren parts of the USSR.

In the 1930s, Stalin pushed the industrialization of his country forward at a furious pace. In the factories, work hours were long and the pay low. The government did not allow workers to change jobs or to move away from their cities. The government's impossibly high production goals, or quotas, affected the quality of goods produced in the Soviet Union. Factory managers took shortcuts to meet their quotas; the result was poor workmanship. Spare parts were in short supply, and no one had time to repair damaged machinery.

Since their pay was fixed by the state, workers had no reason or reward for improving their production. Many stole goods from the factories in order to sell them profitably on the black market. The system of government-set quotas, which Stalin extended to all phases of the Soviet economy, continued well after Stalin was dead. The result, in the 1970s and 1980s, was the gradual breakdown of the Soviet economy.

In order to control this huge Socialist state, in which

the government owned and managed all property, Stalin set up a vast network of police spies. This state police, known as the NKVD, ruled the workers through fear. The police recruited informers to keep a close eye on citizens in every factory, shop, and school. Soviet courts condemned to prison or to a firing squad anyone accused of poor effort or sabotage. Defendants had no right to answer charges or to face their accusers. The arrests of "wreckers," as the police called the accused, climbed into the millions in the 1930s.

The government did not even grant a trial to many wreckers. And it put other, more important, people through public "show trials." The Soviet court system staged these trials and broadcast them to the entire nation. The government told the public that these "enemies of the state" were plotting to bring down the Soviet system. The police arrested most of Stalin's old Bolshevik allies, including Kamenev and Zinoviev. The police tortured these two, and thousands of others, and forced them to sign confessions that the authorities had prepared for them. The Soviet courts then tried, found guilty, and shot these "enemies" of the country. The government allowed no appeals.

Anyone who may have known him before and during the revolution posed a threat to Stalin. He wanted no witnesses to his own past to remain alive. He also wanted unquestioning loyalty from military officers. Older, experienced military men often displayed

*Ramón Mercader,
Trotsky's assassin, in a
Mexican prison in 1950.
He would be released ten
years later.*

independent thinking—a dangerous trait in Stalin's time. Under Stalin's orders, the NKVD executed more than 35,000 officers, including Marshal Mikhail Nikolayevich Tukhachevsky, the head of the Red Army, in the late 1930s.

Stalin even managed to reach out and destroy his most determined enemy—Leon Trotsky. For more than ten years after being thrown out of the Soviet Union, Trotsky traveled in Europe and North America. Eventually, Trotsky settled near Mexico City, where he lived in a closely guarded, walled-in building. There, however, a Spanish-born Mexican named Ramón Mercader, who likely was working under Stalin's orders, murdered Trotsky on the night of August 20, 1940.

Stalin's actions weakened the Soviet Union at an important time. Germany, then under the rule of Adolf Hitler and the Nazi Party, was re-arming itself and enlarging its territory by taking over the land belonging to neighboring countries. To buy time, Stalin made an agreement with Hitler in 1939. This treaty let Stalin invade and conquer part of neighboring Poland and the Baltic states of Estonia, Latvia, and Lithuania. Although he thought that war with Hitler would eventually come, Stalin wanted time to complete the rapid industrialization of the Soviet Union. This would prepare the country for a future war with Germany.

But years of Stalin's type of dictatorship, in which none of his aides dared to question or challenge him, had convinced Stalin that no country could take him by surprise. He assured Soviet citizens that their Red Army could easily defeat any foe. In the summer of 1941, several deserters from the German side crossed into Russia and warned that Hitler was preparing to invade. Stalin, however, was convinced that Hitler wouldn't dare cross the Soviet border.

Stalin was wrong. In the early morning of June 22, 1941, Germany attacked the Soviet Union. Because Soviet forces were completely unprepared, the Germans killed, injured, or took prisoner millions of soldiers that summer. Along the western front, Soviet forces retreated and lost most of their heavy equipment, airplanes, tanks, and artillery.

Worried Soviet men and women in Moscow hear the radio announcement that Nazi Germany has invaded their country.

German soldiers burn the Ukrainian town of Krivoi Rog in 1941.

The war went badly for the Soviet Union. It quickly lost much of western Russia to the Germans. Although he had no military experience, Stalin took personal control of the armed forces. He ordered useless attacks and refused to let Soviet forces retreat. As a result, half of European Russia and many key industrial centers were lost to the Germans. By the winter of 1942, the German army was fighting in the suburbs of Moscow, the capital of the USSR.

The turning point of the war came at Stalingrad, a city on the Volga River. During a fierce winter battle within the city limits, Soviet forces encircled and destroyed a German army of more than 300,000 men. In 1943 the Russians forced the Germans to retreat. Gradually the Red Army prevailed, and by the spring of 1945, the fighting had reached German territory. On April 30, 1945, Hitler committed suicide, and Germany surrendered to the allied forces—Great Britain, the United States, and the Soviet Union—a week later. By

The tide of the war turns for the Soviets at Stalingrad, where these German prisoners are rounded up in February 1943.

British Prime Minister Winston Churchill, U.S. President Franklin Roosevelt, and Soviet Premier Josef Stalin meet to discuss a strategy for defeating Germany and Japan.

At the Potsdam Conference in July 1945, Churchill, Stalin, and new U.S. President Harry Truman (center) decide the fate of a conquered Germany.

then, the Red Army controlled Berlin and much of the eastern part of Germany.

At the war's end, Soviet armies also occupied most of eastern Europe—Hungary, Poland, Czechoslovakia, Romania, Bulgaria, and East Germany. Stalin wanted these nations under his control in order to protect his country against any future invasions. He also needed their markets and industry to help the Soviet Union rebuild after the war. Stalin promised the leaders of the United States and Great Britain that free elections would be held in eastern Europe after the war. But no true elections ever took place. Instead, governments loyal to Stalin and to the USSR were put into power and backed up with Soviet forces.

The new Communist rulers of eastern Europe outlawed all opposing political parties and coordinated their economies with that of the Soviet Union. Stalin, who mistrusted the Western nations, wanted no trade between western and eastern Europe. He also banned foreign newspapers, books, and radio broadcasts. The Soviet Union and the Western countries, including the United States, fell into a bitter and dangerous rivalry that lasted for more than 40 years. This long period of fear and mistrust was called the Cold War.

One country—Yugoslavia—managed to slip out of Soviet control by the late 1940s. Yugoslavia had been created out of six small regions in southeastern Europe after World War I. Josip Broz Tito, who had fought

Josip Broz Tito, the only eastern European leader to remain free of Stalin's tight grip after World War II

against the Germans during World War II, brought the six Yugoslav republics together under his leadership after the war.

Tito favored socialism and, at first, became friends with the Soviet Union. But he insisted on keeping some independence for his country. Stalin, however, allowed no disagreement with his policies and no resistance to his orders, even from close Communist allies. Given this, the two leaders had to clash. When Stalin tried to force Tito into an unfavorable trade agreement with Bulgaria, the Yugoslav leader resisted. Enraged, Stalin forced Yugoslavia from *Cominform*, the organization of eastern European nations, in 1948. Yugoslavia then went its own way as a socialist country—favoring neither the United States nor the Soviet Union.

Stalin saw no reason to make life easier for Soviet citizens after the nation's victory in World War II. In fact, his fear of the West led to higher production quotas and even harsher laws. The arrests of "enemies of the state" continued. The police even arrested, jailed, and, in some cases, executed for treason the returning Soviet soldiers who had been captured and imprisoned by Germany during the war.

In early 1953, Stalin accused the doctors who worked in the Kremlin of conspiring against him and his government. Stalin insisted that the doctors were poisoning government officials. To Soviet citizens, this "doctors' plot" meant only that another harsh purge, or removal of Soviet citizens, was coming. But on March 5—before the secret police could begin making arrests—Stalin died after suffering a stroke. For hours, while he lay helpless on the floor of his country home, no one came to his aid—for no one was allowed to enter his room unannounced, or to summon a doctor. Thus, his mistrust of his closest associates may have contributed to his death.

Stalin was dead, but his harsh reign left a permanent mark on the Soviet Union. In the span of 20 years, Stalin pulled the nation into the modern industrial era, but at the cost of millions of lives. Under Stalin's rule, the Soviet government had become a huge bureaucracy that controlled every aspect of people's lives—where they lived, where they worked, what they could read or discuss. The leaders of this bureaucracy had complete control over the Soviet economy and society.

This system did not represent the ideas of the Russian revolution, which promised that socialism—a society without classes—would replace tsardom—a society of the privileged few and the many poor. Instead of pure socialism, however, Stalin introduced dictatorship, the rule by one person who holds absolute power, like that of the tsar. Not until the 1980s would the socialist dictatorship collapse. Then, socialism crumbled not from outside attack, as Stalin had feared, but from economic failure and a drive for democracy among the people of eastern Europe and the Soviet Union.

3

Nikita Khrushchev

---

*T*he village of Kalinovka lies 225 miles south of Moscow, the capital of the Soviet Union. In the late nineteenth century, Kalinovka was a small and poor village of peasant farmers who lived in mud-walled huts. Many years would pass before these villagers would enjoy such luxuries as paved roads, indoor plumbing, or electricity.

Nikita Sergeyevich Khrushchev was born in a small, thatch-roofed Kalinovka home on April 17, 1894. Khrushchev's family was as poor as its surroundings. His grandfather had been a serf—a farmer who was the property of a landowner and who could be bought and sold as easily as a horse or a plow. Nikita's father, Sergei

Khrushchev, labored as a farm hand but could barely earn a living. Each winter, Sergei left his family to work in the coal mines that lay to the south, in the Donbass region of Ukraine.

Like his father, Nikita Khrushchev was a hard worker. As a young boy, he was responsible for guarding the animals of a wealthy landowner. When he was barely in his teens, he worked in Yuzovka, where his father worked as a miner. In Yuzovka, Nikita cleaned out hot factory boilers, a dirty and dangerous job.

Eventually, Sergei decided that he should move his family away from Kalinovka. In 1908, when Nikita was 14, the entire family moved to Yuzovka. There Nikita found work at a factory. He had good mechanical skills and quickly learned how to repair the factory's complicated machines. His ability set him apart from many of the older men who performed simple labor in Yuzovka's mines and factories.

Nikita also quickly learned to read and write at schools in Kalinovka and Yuzovka. He studied the works of the great novelists and thinkers of his day. While still a teenager, he read the *Communist Manifesto* by Karl Marx and Friedrich Engels. This small book, which called for a revolution of the world's industrial workers, made a great impression on the young mechanic.

In 1913, a wave of strikes and demonstrations erupted among the workers in Yuzovka. When Nikita Khrushchev joined the strike, the police quickly arrested him. Although he lost his job, Khrushchev quickly found another at the nearby Rutchenkovo mine. His mechanical skill impressed the mine bosses, who gave him the important job of maintaining the elevators that carried miners into and out of the deep coal mines.

In 1914 war erupted between Germany and Russia. Although many miners had to join the army, the Rutchenkovo mines needed Khrushchev's skills. The military draft allowed him to stay in Yuzovka.

The war went badly for Russia, which suffered complete defeat at the hands of the German forces. More than six million Russian soldiers were killed. Angry at the tsar and at their government for this disaster, workers throughout Russia took part in violent demonstrations in 1915. Two years later, the Russian government collapsed after a massive strike in the capital of Petrograd.

Suddenly, in the spring of 1917, no one in the towns and villages of the Donbass region had any authority. So, Khrushchev and several colleagues organized a soviet—a worker's council—to run the towns and to organize a militia for defense. Later, in the fall of 1917, Lenin and the Bolsheviks took control of the Russian government.

Despite the Bolsheviks' success, many people in Yuzovka, and throughout Russia, opposed Lenin and his party. In 1918 a civil war broke out between the Red Guards—the Bolshevik army—and the Whites—the army representing the tsarist government. Leaders in Ukraine took the opportunity to declare their region an independent country, free from the socialist government established by the Bolsheviks. In March, a German army invaded Ukraine to drive out the Bolsheviks.

Khrushchev, like many other miners in the region, supported the Bolsheviks. In 1917 he joined the Red Guards. But in the next year German forces overran the Red Guards in Ukraine, forcing Khrushchev to flee his native village of Kalinovka.

Wherever he went, Nikita Khrushchev became a leader. He soon returned to Kalinovka, where he organized the peasants into a new soviet. The peasants seized the land they had worked for generations and divided it among themselves. In April 1918, Khrushchev decided to join the Bolshevik party.

The civil war continued for several years. The conflict was confusing, with White and Red armies attacking and retreating in all directions and leaving both farms and villages in ruins. Khrushchev became a political *commissar*—an officer responsible for keeping up morale and preventing desertion. Despite miserable and dangerous conditions, Khrushchev kept the soldiers of his unit in line. He also took part in many of the fiercest battles of the civil war.

In 1920, the war came to an end. It was won by the Bolsheviks. But times were hard, for the armies had destroyed many industries throughout the country. If the factories and mines did not reopen, the country's economy would collapse. Khrushchev returned to Yuzovka to restore the mines to full production. As in the Red Guards, Khrushchev became a commissar. This time he struggled with hunger as well as desertion. In addition, bandits and anti-Bolshevik guerrillas made hit-and-run attacks on the mines. Some of Khrushchev's closest colleagues were killed in these skirmishes.

The Russian economy, which had been completely taken over by the Bolsheviks, was backwards and inefficient. Many people found that, under the Bolsheviks, life had not improved. Food was scarce, and work in the factories and mines was poorly paid. Despite these hardships, Khrushchev worked hard to inspire the miners. He often gave speeches, asking them to work long hours in the pits for low pay. He was completely dedicated to the Bolshevik cause and saw himself as an important part of building the new socialist state in Russia.

Although he was offered a promotion in 1922, Khrushchev did not accept it. He was an ambitious man, and he wanted to move further up the Party ladder. He enrolled in the Yuzovka Workers Faculty, a school for young Bolshevik officials. At the school, he kept a close watch on his fellow students, guiding them in the official policies of the central government. Upon his graduation in 1925, Khrushchev became the secretary (Party leader) of a district near Yuzovka, which had been renamed Stalino.

The man for whom Yuzovka was renamed—Josef Stalin—was struggling to defeat his rivals after the death of Vladimir Lenin in 1924. To win power, Stalin needed the help of younger members of the Communist party like Khrushchev. In return for their help, he promoted them to more important Party jobs. Khrushchev remained strongly loyal to Stalin, and for this, he would be well rewarded in the future.

While working in his district in the late 1920s, Khrushchev made important friendships with the Communist leaders of Ukraine. He became a delegate to a congress of the Ukrainian Communist Party in

An avid outdoorsman, Nikita Khrushchev takes a break from his leadership duties to go fishing.

1925 and a non-voting delegate to the All-Union Congress in Moscow in December 1925. Khrushchev's hard work and ability attracted the attention of Lazar Kaganovich, the head of the Ukrainian Communist Party. Through the help of Kaganovich, Khrushchev attained increasingly important positions in Ukraine.

Kaganovich, who became an important aide and partner, or ally, of Josef Stalin, brought Khrushchev to Moscow, where the young commissar enrolled in the Stalin Industrial Academy. By this time, Stalin firmly controlled Russia. Still a young man, Khrushchev was now working in Moscow and would witness firsthand the events of Stalin's rule.

Although the government had established the Stalin Industrial Academy to train factory managers, Khrushchev's goal at the school was to gain further contacts and power within the Communist party. His first step was to help defeat opponents of Stalin who had won an election for leadership of the students' Party organization. Khrushchev was elected the new head when another vote was taken. He then expelled his opponents.

In 1931 Khrushchev became Party leader in two of the most important districts in Moscow—the Bauman and the Red Presnya neighborhoods. He supervised local factory workers, pushing them to produce more while also cutting their wages. He set up a system that punished any worker who arrived late for work or who did not produce enough; forced others out of their jobs; and jailed others.

By 1935 Nikita Khrushchev became first secretary of the Moscow Party Committee—the boss of Moscow. He also joined the Central Committee of the Communist party. He was given responsibility for the construction of the Moscow subway system, one of the biggest public projects in Soviet history.

By the mid-1930s, Stalin's extensive purges had eliminated many officials around Khrushchev. Some were executed; others were deported to Siberia, never to be seen again. Khrushchev remained loyal to Stalin throughout the worst years of the purges. Stalin rewarded him with a non-voting seat on the Politburo, the most powerful ruling council in the country. In 1938 Khrushchev also became first secretary of the Ukrainian Communist Party.

In the republic of Ukraine, Khrushchev's task was to stop Ukrainian resistance to central rule by Moscow. Khrushchev first purged opponents within the Ukrainian party. He then worked to "Russify" the region by forcing schools to teach the Russian language instead of Ukrainian, and by arresting many Ukrainian teachers and writers. At this time, agricultural and industrial production in Ukraine was increasing. Khrushchev's success in governing this huge territory landed him a position as a voting, or full, member of the Politburo.

In 1939 the Soviet Union began to prepare for war. Under Adolf Hitler, Germany invaded many of its neighboring countries. A secret pact between Stalin and Hitler kept the Soviet Union temporarily out of the world war that erupted when German armies invaded Poland in 1939. As part of this deal, Hitler and Stalin agreed to share Poland's territory. Stalin appointed the most important Party official in the Ukraine—Khrushchev—to the task of transforming eastern Poland into "western Ukraine." Krushchev brought in Soviet newspapers, arrested Poles opposed to "sovietization," and arranged elections that Communist officials easily won. These officials later voted to annex the new territory to the Soviet Union officially. By 1940 the nation of Poland had completely disappeared.

The pact signed by Hitler and Stalin did not prevent war between the two nations, however. In June 1941, German forces lined up along the new German-Soviet border in preparation for a massive invasion of the Soviet Union. On June 21, Khrushchev received word from a German deserter of a coming attack. Despite Khrushchev's personal call to Stalin, the Soviet leader ignored the warning. On June 22, 1941, war broke out between Germany and the Soviet Union.

The Red Army was completely unprepared to fight the Germans. Millions of people died during the war, which became a desperate struggle for survival for the

Ukrainians. Many people in Ukraine welcomed the Germans, whom they thought would free them from Stalin's harsh rule. Khrushchev took part in many important battles, including the winter battle of Stalingrad. Here the Russian soldiers encircled and annihilated an entire German army group. After Stalingrad, the tide turned against the German forces. The Russians drove them from Kiev, the Ukrainian capital, in the fall of 1943. Khrushchev entered the ruined city with an assignment to restore order and to rebuild industry. Stalin appointed him head of the Ukrainian government.

At this time, many Ukrainians still fought against Russian control of their land. Guerrilla groups attacked Red Army units. The conflict further damaged the Ukrainian economy. By 1946, after the war with Germany had been over for a year, Ukraine—which had the Soviet Union's most fertile and productive land—was going through a terrible famine.

Khrushchev appealed to Stalin for food. But the dictator denied the request. Instead, the central government took all the available grain out of the region. Because of his efforts to feed the Ukrainians, Khrushchev was replaced in the spring of 1947 by Kaganovich. Stalin felt that Khrushchev had not been tough enough in reorganizing the collective farms of the Ukraine after the war.

The war and its aftermath had a strong effect on Nikita Khrushchev. He had seen firsthand the hunger, destruction, and suffering caused by Stalin's harsh policies and poor decisions. He had also seen millions of Ukrainians greet an invading foreign army—the Germans—as liberators. Although he could not express his feelings in public, he began to doubt the leadership of the man to whom he had devoted so much of his energy and ability during the past 20 years.

The Soviet leader restored Khrushchev as boss of Ukraine in 1947. But Khrushchev did not remain in Kiev for long. Through new purges Stalin had killed and exiled many members of the Russian leadership. One of the leaders of these post-war purges was Georgy Malenkov. He became one of Khrushchev's rivals. Seeing Malenkov's power and importance on the rise, Stalin brought Khrushchev to Moscow. Stalin hoped to play the two men off against each other. In this way, Stalin thought he could control both men.

During his years in politics, Khrushchev made many strong allies within the Soviet government. Arriving in Moscow, however, he began competing with Malenkov. The two of them were caught in the political schemes that revolved around Stalin, who was becoming increasingly paranoid. Stalin mistrusted all his aides and often accused the people around him of plotting his death.

In March 1953, Stalin suffered a stroke and died. He had not prepared a successor, and the Soviet Union

Though favored by many Soviets—including Stalin, to whom he was a close aide—Georgy Malenkov struggled with Khrushchev for control of the Party.

suddenly had no leader. At a meeting in the Kremlin, Stalin's aides appointed Malenkov as premier. Lavrenty Beria, Stalin's chief of secret police, and Vyacheslav Molotov, the Soviet foreign minister, also gained powerful positions. But a week later Malenkov was forced to give up his post as senior Party secretary in favor of Khrushchev.

Khrushchev then moved carefully against Beria, who controlled an independent and very dangerous network of police agents. To deal with Beria, Khrushchev called on his ally Marshal Georgy Zhukov, a Russian World War II hero. Zhukov moved tanks and troops into Moscow and surrounded the Kremlin. Khrushchev then called a meeting of top officials. He condemned

Beria, and called in a group of military officers to arrest him. Later, the government tried and executed Beria. His fall from power brought an end to the independence of the Soviet secret police.

Malenkov and Khrushchev now fought with each other for control of the Soviet state. They battled with speeches, articles, and policies. In 1954 Khrushchev planned to increase Soviet food production by planting millions of acres of land in arid regions of central Asia. He went into the countryside and persuaded local Communist officials to support him. Khrushchev fired officials who opposed him and appointed in their place loyal men who would willingly follow his instructions.

Marshal Georgy Zhukov (standing at table), the World War II hero who defeated the Germans at Stalingrad, backed Khrushchev in his rivalry with Malenkov, but later had a falling out with him.

Khrushchev (center) with Nikolai Bulganin (left), the former mayor of Moscow and defense minister under Stalin

Khrushchev's plan succeeded. That year the country produced good harvests. In Feburary 1955, Malenkov, who had opposed the plan, resigned as premier. Nikolai Bulganin replaced him.

Over the next few years, sweeping changes in the political system of the Soviet Union occurred. Stalin's reputation began to fade as writers openly discussed the trials, purges, and executions that occurred in the 1930s. Perhaps the most important single event during this period was Khrushchev's own "secret speech." He gave this speech to a closed meeting of the Communist party in 1956.

The speech stunned Party members who heard it. For four and one-half hours, Khrushchev spoke of Stalin's brutal methods in great detail. He also claimed that Stalin had betrayed the ideas of socialism. Khrushchev maintained that Stalin's methods had left Russia too weak to put up a good fight against the Germans in 1941. Khrushchev gave this speech because he wanted to pave the way for reforms of the Soviet system. He knew that "destalinization," that is, discrediting Stalin and his policies, would never succeed if the official government policy toward Stalin did not change.

The "secret speech" caused upheavals in the Soviet Union and in eastern Europe. Riots broke out in Soviet Georgia and in Poland, which had become a Communist nation after World War II. Hungary revolted against Communist control. In response, Khrushchev and Malenkov ordered the Soviet army to invade Hungary. Russian soldiers killed thousands of Hungarians in the fighting. This happened despite the fact that Yuri Andropov, the Russian ambassador, had assured the Hungarians that no invasion would take place.

These events threatened Khrushchev's position. His "destalinization" seemed to weaken the hold the Communist party had on the country. In addition, he had attempted to reorganize the government departments responsible for running the economy. This action turned many of Khrushchev's colleagues against him.

At a meeting in 1957, Malenkov, Molotov, and Bulganin voted Khrushchev out of the government. But Khrushchev was too smart for his enemies. He insisted that the Central Committee vote on his future. After the Central Committee supported Khrushchev, Malenkov and Molotov resigned from their government posts.

In March 1958, Khrushchev replaced Bulganin as premier. Now Khrushchev was both premier and general secretary. With the top jobs in both the Soviet government and in the Party, Khrushchev was the uncontested leader of the Soviet Union.

Despite his high rank, Khrushchev still traveled all over the USSR, visiting mines, factories, and farms. He also traveled abroad. He met with the leaders of France, China, and the United States. On one journey to the United States, he saw California, New York, Iowa, and Pittsburgh. But much to Khrushchev's surprise and anger, the government of the United States did not permit him to visit Disneyland.

Khrushchev had many ideas on how to increase the amount of food the Soviet Union was producing. He wanted Soviet farms to surpass the United States in the amount of meat, milk, and butter raised or produced for the general population. But his eagerness to meet these goals quickly led to some irresponsible and unworkable ideas. One of these ideas was growing corn—a crop not suited to the soil or climate of the Soviet Union. Thus, Khrushchev's plan harmed the nation's economy.

Khrushchev made these plans because he hoped to improve his country's standard of living. The people of the Soviet Union lacked many everyday comforts that

Touring America's agricultural heartland, Khrushchev makes a speech in an Iowa cornfield.

people in the West took for granted, such as shoes, clothing, cars, and kitchen appliances. In addition, many kinds of food were scarce and expensive. Khrushchev used his own popularity among the Soviet people to pressure officials to agree with his plans and goals. This caused many officials, who lived quite well themselves, to turn against their leader.

Khrushchev continued to accuse the late Josef Stalin

of terrible crimes. At a meeting of the 22nd Party Congress in October 1961, Khrushchev once again denounced, or spoke against, the man who had guided the early years of his life. This time, many others, including a young delegate in attendance named Mikhail Gorbachev, shared Khrushchev's views. Khrushchev and Gorbachev voted to move Stalin's body, which lay beside that of Lenin, to an ordinary grave.

In the early 1960s Khrushchev stood at the height of his popularity within the Soviet Union. The country's success in launching Sputnik, the first orbital satellite, seemed to reflect the great advances made since the Russian revolution. Stalin's reign of fear was only a memory, and newly independent countries around the world were turning to the Soviet Union for guidance.

Khrushchev, who felt that no one in the Communist party would seriously oppose him, began proposing even more radical agricultural reforms. Soon, he banned private gardening plots. Farmers had used these to grow food for themselves and for sale on private markets. The Soviet government now told farmers exactly how much of each crop to grow. This central planning proved inefficient. Khrushchev eventually had to return private plots to Soviet farmers.

Natural disasters also kept Khrushchev's plans from being realized. Cool weather reduced the corn crop in the European part of Russia in 1962. In 1963 a severe

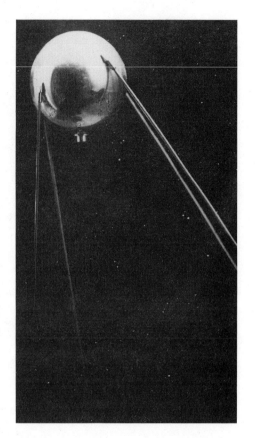

Sputnik, the first artificial satellite, seemed to symbolize Soviet technological progress. Its launch on October 4, 1957, marked the beginning of more than 30 years of Soviet-American competition for supremacy in space.

drought in Asia spoiled crops in Kazakhstan. The result was rising food prices and shortages. Strikes and protests occurred in many Soviet cities. In 1963 the Soviet Union had to buy grain from foreign countries for the first time in its history, in order to feed its people. This humiliated Khrushchev, who prided himself on his agricultural knowledge and who claimed that the USSR would one day be as wealthy as the United States.

About this time, Khrushchev also began to have

Fidel Castro (seated) took power in Cuba on January 1, 1959. A self-described Marxist-Leninist, he received much military and economic aid from the Soviet Union.

problems with his own Communist allies. China, which was ruled by leaders still loyal to the ideas of Stalin, exploded its first nuclear weapon in 1964. Mao Tse-tung, the Chinese leader, openly opposed Khrushchev and claimed to be the true leader of the world's socialist countries. Both the Soviet Union and China sent large armies to their borders and became bitter and dangerous rivals.

Another allied socialist state was the island nation of Cuba, which lay just 60 miles off the coast of Florida.

In an attempt to overthrow the socialist Cuban government, the United States invaded the island. The invasion failed, but Khrushchev felt that he had to protect
the Cuban government from any further attack. He
ordered nuclear warheads and missiles to be sent to
Cuba. This action, he hoped, would make up for
Russia's inability to protect Cuba because of the distance
involved.

After U.S. President John Kennedy was shown photographs of the silos that were to house these new missiles, the two superpowers engaged in a showdown.
Kennedy announced a total naval blockade of Cuba.
The United States and the Soviet Union came danger-
ously close to war.

Khrushchev's own military wanted to risk a war. But
Khrushchev realized that Kennedy would never accept
the presence of Soviet missiles in Cuba. He offered a
deal that would save face on both sides: the Soviet
Union would remove the missiles if Kennedy would
agree not to invade Cuba. The two countries made the
deal. As a secret part of the pact, Kennedy agreed that
the United States would later pull missiles out of
Turkey, a country that bordered the Soviet Union on
the south.

Although Khrushchev had avoided war with the
United States, he was now in trouble in the Soviet
Union. Many thought he had needlessly backed down
and humiliated the country. Others opposed his plans

Photographic evidence such as this convinced President John F. Kennedy that Soviet missiles in Cuba threatened the United States.

Kennedy's confrontation with Khrushchev (seated together below), known as the Cuban missile crisis, brought the United States and the USSR to the brink of nuclear war.

for reform of the Soviet system. Industrial production had improved. But many Soviet citizens still suffered through shortages of food and consumer goods. Blame for the country's problems rested squarely on Khrushchev's shoulders.

One of Khrushchev's ideas caused a near breakdown in the country's administration. In 1961 he had decided that the Communist party should be divided in two, with one branch handling industry and the other agriculture. This angered many Party members. They were uncertain as to who was in charge in the country's many administrative districts. Within a short time, Khrushchev, amid much criticism of his leadership, had to discard the idea.

Soon many powerful Communist officials were plotting among themselves to replace Khrushchev. In October 1964, while Khrushchev was spending time at his vacation home on the Black Sea, he received an urgent phone call. The caller told him to return to Moscow immediately for a meeting.

Khrushchev, who knew there was no pressing business to discuss, realized that he was in trouble. When he arrived at the *Presidium* meeting, he found that only one member would support him. Khrushchev appealed for help from the Central Committee, but the plotters had prevented Khrushchev's supporters from attending a special session of the committee. Instead of putting up a fight, the 70-year-old Khrushchev resigned on

October 14. Leonid Brezhnev replaced him as general secretary of the Communist party, and Aleksy Kosygin became premier.

Khrushchev retired to a country house, where he spent the rest of his life writing, reading, and pursuing his many hobbies. He worked in a small garden, talked with farmers who lived nearby, and wrote a book about his life. He died in 1971 at the age of 77.

Although Nikita Khrushchev's reign as the leader of the Soviet Union was short, he ruled during an important time in the country's history. In the late 1950s and early 1960s, the Soviet economy expanded, providing a better life for the nation's people. Khrushchev achieved this without using the force and terror of Stalin.

Khrushchev's own fall from power was a peaceful one. By condemning Stalinism, he reshaped the Party to allow a political—and not violent—change in leadership. Yet he had learned that members of the Communist bureaucracy would join forces to resist any change and to protect their interests. Khrushchev's experience was a valuable lesson for many future Soviet reformers, including Mikhail Gorbachev.

4

Leonid Brezhnev

*B*y the first decade of the twentieth century, industrialization was changing cities and towns throughout the Russian Empire. Factories, mines, and mills employed a growing class of industrial workers. In 1917 these workers, led by Vladimir Lenin and the Bolshevik party, brought down the empire and helped to create the Soviet Union. Without the support of factory laborers, Lenin would never have succeeded in seizing power in Russia.

Leonid Ilyich Brezhnev, who succeeded Nikita Khrushchev as general secretary of the Communist party, was the first Soviet leader who came from the urban working class. Born in 1906, Brezhnev grew up in a one-room house in the Ukrainian town of Kamenskoye. Four generations of Brezhnevs—who were from the Russian Republic

Leonid Ilyich Brezhnev (center), waves from atop Lenin's tomb in Red Square, where Soviet leaders traditionally greeted the people on November 7 to celebrate the Bolshevik seizure of power. With Brezhnev are Edward Gierek, first secretary of the Polish Communist Party and Aleksy Kosygin (right), the Soviet premier.

and not the Ukrainian—had been steelworkers and city dwellers. Nevertheless, Leonid Brezhnev experienced a childhood as poor as that of many Russian peasants.

Determined to provide him with a better future, Leonid's parents paid his tuition to a local boys' college, which he entered in 1915. By then, war with Germany was raging in the western part of the Russian Empire and in Ukraine. Losses at the front and food shortages at home caused strikes and rioting among the Russian workers. However, the Brezhnev family stayed out of politics and didn't take sides in the civil war that later destroyed much of Ukraine. Brezhnev remained in school throughout that confusing period, when many families in Kamenskoye fled to the east or tried to leave the country. Only 15 members of his school class, out of an original 40, managed to graduate with him in 1921.

In 1923, Brezhnev entered a vocational school to study metallurgy (the science of working metals). In the same year, he joined the *Komsomol*, or Communist Union of Youth. This organization trained young people to become loyal Communist party members. The Komsomol was also the first step on the ladder to a career within the Soviet government.

Brezhnev continued his studies at the Kursk Land Technicum, a school that prepared students to survey land and to manage state farms. After graduating in 1927, he went to Byelorussia, in the western Soviet Union, to carry out Stalin's drive to "collectivize" peasant farmers. His job was to seize private farmlands and organize them into collective farms under government direction. On these farms, the laborers would own the land in common and would be responsible for raising a certain amount of food. The government would then buy the food at fixed prices.

In Byelorussia, Brezhnev and his colleagues tried to persuade the local peasants to leave their land and join the collective farms. Some peasants agreed to work on them; others refused. If necessary, Brezhnev used force. He arrested, and in some cases executed, peasants who resisted collectivization.

Thus, Brezhnev began his slow but steady rise within the Communist bureaucracy. Under Stalin's rule, older members of the Party were forced out of their jobs. Stalin imprisoned, exiled, or sentenced to death many loyal Bolsheviks who had fought in the revolution of 1917. Brezhnev and other young officials then stepped into the jobs left vacant. Thankful for the opportunity Stalin's purges offered him, Brezhnev remained loyal throughout his life to the Soviet dictator's methods and ideas.

Brezhnev's work in Byelorussia earned him a nomination as a candidate—or non-voting—member of the Communist party in 1930. Although enrolled in the Moscow Agricultural Academy, he left the capital and returned to his home town of Kamenskoye. Brezhnev realized that the easiest route to success lay outside Moscow. He had little chance for advancement within the Party's huge central bureaucracy. In Ukraine, however, he could build alliances with local Party leaders and wait for a chance to land a better job with the guidance of these friends.

In Kamenskoye, Brezhnev worked in a local mill as an oiler and later as a machinist. He had no intention of spending his life within the factory gates, however. He soon applied to and was accepted at the Arsenichov

Metallurgical Institute. There he became the Communist party secretary, overseeing the organization and activities of the party members at the school. He was also assigned the task of organizing groups of Komsomol members to seize food from Ukrainian peasants and force them onto collective farms.

Brezhnev graduated from the Arsenichov institute in 1935. Two years later, he was nominated to run for deputy town mayor of Kamenskoye. Brezhnev had no need to campaign for this office. The Party, which appointed only one candidate, arranged elections in the Soviet Union. Brezhnev and other town officials were then elected by a unanimous vote.

In this, his first important government job, Brezhnev proved himself both loyal and hardworking. He found a powerful friend in Nikita Khrushchev, who was then the boss of the Ukrainian Communist Party. Under Khrushchev, Brezhnev was later appointed secretary for propaganda in Ukraine's Dnepropetrovsk region. Given control of local newspapers, he kept a close eye on public meetings and conferences. The secretary had to support the Stalinist system and make the local Party boss, Khrushchev, look good. Brezhnev also played an important role in the "Russification" of the region. That is, he replaced the Ukrainian language with Russian—the language of business and government—and required all students to study the Russian language in the public schools.

The factories and mines of Ukraine were important to the rapid industrialization then taking place in the Soviet Union. In 1941 Stalin, convinced that war was coming, ordered the factories in Ukraine to make weapons. To direct this operation, Stalin appointed Brezhnev as defense minister in Dnepropetrovsk. Under his management, old steel factories in the region turned out tanks, guns, and shells at a furious pace.

But World War II was coming faster than anyone suspected. After the Germans attacked in June 1941, the Soviets quickly took apart their factories. The Russians moved the factories to the east, beyond the reach of the German armies that were marching across southern Russia and Ukraine. In July, Brezhnev joined the Red Army, and in the spring of 1942, he became one of the army's political commissars. As a commissar, he kept up morale in his unit and punished disloyalty and desertion. Army officials assigned him to the 18th Army, which fought in southern Russia, Ukraine, and eastern Europe.

In 1945, as the Red Army swept westwards towards Germany, the 18th Army entered the regions of Transcarpathia—a part of Romania—and Czechoslovakia. Despite the promises to his Western allies, however, Stalin did not intend to liberate these areas. Instead, in the spring and summer of 1945, he assigned commissars like Brezhnev to arrange elections in eastern Europe that would bring loyal Communists to power.

Soviet Foreign Minister Vyacheslav Molotov, here turning toward Stalin (center) at the Potsdam Conference, helped to administer the Party purges of the 1930s that would allow Leonid Brezhnev and other young Communists to rise to power.

To increase popular support for Communist rule, Brezhnev promised land reforms and democratic elections to the people of Czechoslovakia. When persuasion didn't work, he simply arrested opponents and sent them into exile. He rigged elections to favor Soviet loyalists, and forced the country's leaders to follow Stalin's lead in economic and foreign affairs. Trade with western Europe was cut off, and Czechoslovakia became a satellite state of the Soviet Union.

In 1946 Brezhnev returned to civilian life and to Ukraine. War had wasted the region, and many of the largest Ukrainian cities lay in ruins. The government gave Brezhnev control of an important project—the rebuilding of a huge steelworks in the Zaporozhye region. He drove the workers hard and got assembly lines going ahead of schedule in the fall of 1947. Josef Stalin publicly praised Brezhnev and awarded him a medal for his efforts.

In the early 1950s, Brezhnev became the Communist party boss of Moldavia, a region near Romania that had been brought under Soviet control in 1940. His new job was not an easy one, however. The people of Moldavia resisted Soviet rule and demanded independence. To enforce the collectivization and Russification of Moldavia, Brezhnev established harsh policies. There he also met Konstantin Chernenko, an official from Ukraine who became Brezhnev's close friend and ally.

After silencing opposition and bringing Moldavia under Soviet control, Brezhnev was elected to the Central Committee of the Communist party in 1952. His loyalty to Stalin and his willingness to carry out Stalin's programs had finally brought him power in the Soviet capital.

Stalin's death in 1953, however, threw the Party into great confusion. Some of Stalin's policies were changed and Brezhnev, as a loyal Stalinist, was fired from his posts. Khrushchev's rivalry with Malenkov for the Soviet leadership placed Brezhnev's own future in jeopardy.

Success within the Soviet system depended on making friendships and partnerships with powerful leaders. As a young Communist official in the 1930s, Brezhnev had been frequently promoted by Khrushchev and had carried out Khrushchev's policies. His future depended on Khrushchev, who wanted to defeat Malenkov and gain control of Soviet government.

To expand agricultural production, Khrushchev designed an ambitious program in Kazakhstan. He opened up the vast, arid lands of this central Asian region to grain farmers from other parts of the Soviet Union. To put his program in place and to make sure it wouldn't fail, Khrushchev appointed Brezhnev as second secretary of the Communist party of Kazakhstan.

Brezhnev arrived at Alma-Ata, the capital of Kazakhstan, in February 1954. The most challenging task of his career—to build up a successful agricultural program from scratch—faced him. Kazakhstan's thin soil and unpredictable weather made growing crops difficult. In addition, the transportation and distribution system in the region was old-fashioned.

Despite these problems, the first year produced a good crop. Khrushchev promoted Brezhnev to the post of first secretary of Kazakhstan after the successful harvests were announced. Soon afterwards, Malenkov, who had opposed Khrushchev's program, resigned from the Presidium—the ruling council that had been known as the Politburo under Stalin. As general secretary of the

Yugoslavia's Marshal Tito, here visiting with Khrushchev (right) in the USSR, remained faithful to the Communist cause as Brezhnev struggled to keep other eastern European leaders in the Soviet camp.

Communist party, Khrushchev was now the "first among equals"—the most powerful official in the Soviet Union.

By 1956 Khrushchev was ready to begin his unexpected reforms in the Soviet system. Seeking to shake up the Party, he delivered his famous "secret speech," in which he criticized Stalin's purges and harsh dictatorship. Khrushchev's opinions shocked many Party members, both inside and outside the Soviet Union. Some eastern European Communist leaders saw the speech as a signal that they no longer had to follow Moscow's lead. Brezhnev was responsible for keeping eastern Europe under Soviet control. So, when a revolt against

Soviet rule broke out in Hungary in 1956, Brezhnev and a close ally, Yuri Andropov (the Soviet ambassador to Hungary), crushed the revolt with a force of Soviet tanks and troops.

After Brezhnev put down the revolt in Hungary, Khrushchev gave him control of the Soviet Union's space research and nuclear weapons programs. To the Soviet leadership, the "space race" was the most important symbol of their competition with the Western countries, particularly with the United States. In addition, the Cold War, which began after World War II, was causing an intense rivalry between the Soviet government and the United States. Brezhnev's job was to make sure the Soviet Union did not fall behind the United States in the building of nuclear weapons. He became an expert in military affairs and an important link between the Soviet armed forces and the civilian government.

In the early 1960s, Brezhnev also forged close ties with smaller countries in Africa and Asia. Many of these nations had recently won their independence from European countries. They were eager to ally with the Soviet Union, which promised financial aid and a detailed plan for creating a socialist state. A skilled diplomat, Brezhnev brought the Soviet Union new allies and influence in many corners of the globe.

Brezhnev, however, was loyal to the Communist system and disagreed with many of the reforms that Nikita

Khrushchev attempted. When Khrushchev reached an agreement with the United States over the divided German city of Berlin, Brezhnev felt that the Soviet leader was giving in to the West. He also differed with Khrushchev over the Cuban missile crisis of 1962, when Khrushchev agreed to close down missile sites on the island of Cuba. Although he could not publicly criticize his leader, Brezhnev allied himself with Mikhail Suslov, a powerful member of the Presidium who strongly opposed Khrushchev.

In 1964 Suslov and other members of the Presidium forced Khrushchev to resign his office. By expressing no support for Khrushchev's ideas in public, Brezhnev established himself as an independent. Suslov, who did not seek the leadership for himself, supported Brezhnev as Khrushchev's successor. Promising that Party officials

Mikhail Suslov, known as the Communist party's leading theoretician, or hardliner, supported Khrushchev in the 1950s, but later opposed him in favor of Brezhnev.

would keep their traditional privileges, Brezhnev replaced his rivals within the government with officials who supported him. By 1966, his position as leader of the Party and of the country was secure.

During the next few years, Brezhnev dismantled many of the Party reforms introduced by Khrushchev. To improve his grip on the *KGB*, the Soviet state police, he put Yuri Andropov in charge of the organization in 1967. Konstantin Chernenko, his colleague from Moldavia, was promoted to the Presidium (which Brezhnev had renamed the Politburo).

The Communist bureaucracy flourished during Brezhnev's term. He rewarded Communist officials who were loyal to him with lifetime jobs and advancement. The result was the creation of a privileged class of Soviet bureaucrats who benefited from the *nomenklatura* system. The members of this class enjoyed a special status within the Soviet state. They could rent spacious apartments and shop at well-stocked government stores. They could easily buy cars, telephones, appliances, and vacation homes. Their children attended private schools. Thus the nomenklatura system of appointments to the best positions and jobs allowed a few people to be protected from many of the everyday hardships and shortages suffered by ordinary Soviet citizens.

But Khrushchev's attempted reforms had also brought new freedom to Soviet writers and artists. Many of these openly criticized the Communist system.

Andrei Sakharov, winner of the 1975 Nobel Peace Prize, led the movement for human rights in the Soviet Union during the Brezhnev years and beyond.

Brezhnev no longer allowed these dissidents to publish their novels or stage their plays. He jailed or exiled many of them. These policies forced Alexander Solzhenitsyn, the author of many well-known dissident works, to move to the United States. The government sent Andrei Sakharov, a physicist who had helped develop the Soviet hydrogen bomb, to the city of Gorky, where he lived in isolation.

Brezhnev also dealt harshly with eastern European nations that stepped out of line. He announced that the Soviet Union and its allies were dependent on each other to keep their loyalty to socialism. In practice, this "Brezhnev Doctrine" meant that the Soviet Union could interfere if a socialist ally moved away from Soviet control.

Brezhnev put this idea into practice in 1968.

Alexander Dubcek, the leader of the Communist party in Czechoslovakia, was making sweeping reforms in his country. (Brezhnev had helped bring this country into the Soviet *bloc* in 1945.) Dubcek allowed secret elections and opposition parties in Czechoslovakia. He also relaxed censorship of newspapers and television.

Brezhnev opposed these reforms and decided to make an example of Dubcek. Tanks of the Soviet Union and of other eastern European nations invaded the Czechoslovakian capital of Prague in August 1968. A few days of bloody street battles put an end to Dubcek's government.

Although the Brezhnev Doctrine helped the Soviet Union to keep a tight grip on its socialist allies, the Soviet Union itself was suffering from economic stagnation. The problem originated with the Soviet system of central planning. With this system, the government set all production goals over a period of several years. To make their production quotas, factory managers used poor materials and inefficient production methods. Workers, all of whom made roughly the same wage, had no reason to work harder, since their pay did not improve. Brezhnev's military buildup drained the Soviet treasury, and collective farms failed to produce enough food to meet demand.

Brezhnev saw a possible solution to these problems: he would relax tensions with the West and with the United States. Thus began the new policy of détente—

an improvement of relations between the Soviet Union and the West. Brezhnev believed that with increased diplomatic and economic contacts, the Soviet Union would gain access to Western technology. At the same time, the high military spending that was draining the Soviet economy would diminish.

In May 1972, Brezhnev met with U.S. President Richard Nixon in Moscow. The two leaders signed a treaty at the Strategic Arms Limitation Talks (SALT). This treaty limited the number of intercontinental nuclear missiles deployed by the two nations. Three

U. S. President Gerald R. Ford with Brezhnev in the Soviet city of Vladivostok, in November 1974. The American architect of détente, Secretary of State Henry Kissinger, stands directly behind Ford.

years later, the leaders of western Europe and the Soviet Union met in Helsinki, Finland. The Western powers officially agreed to recognize the territorial gains the Soviet Union had made after World War II. Another part of the treaty stated that all countries signing the pact must allow their citizens free speech and the right to emigrate, or move away from their home country. After the Helsinki accords, many groups arose within the Soviet Union to make sure the nation obeyed the treaty. Brezhnev and the Communist party, however, had no intention of allowing free speech or public criticism. In fact, the government continued to arrest dissidents and refused to allow many Soviet citizens to emigrate.

Brezhnev signed another SALT treaty with U.S. President Jimmy Carter in 1979. To some extent, détente seemed to be healing the Soviet economy and improving the Soviet Union's image abroad. In the same year, however, a rivalry between two Communist parties in the central Asian nation of Afghanistan prompted the Soviet leadership to order the invasion of that country. The United Nations and the United States condemned the war in Afghanistan. To show its disapproval of the war, the U.S. government cut off grain sales to the Soviet Union, and President Carter forced the U.S. Olympic team to boycott the Summer Olympics of 1980, which were held in Moscow.

Brezhnev's problems mounted in the early 1980s.

In June 1979, Brezhnev signed the SALT II treaty with U.S. President Jimmy Carter, who later that year would strongly criticize Brezhnev for the Soviet invasion of Afghanistan (below).

He was unable to stop the rapid changes in communications, which were making many Soviet and eastern European citizens aware of their relatively poor standard of living. But the Communist party could not reform the economy without allowing new freedoms and losing its tight hold on Soviet citizens. In addition, the people who approved of the nomenklatura system and were managing cities and industries opposed any reform of that system. Corruption, bribery, and incompetence increased at all levels of the country's management. Grain harvests continued to decline, and the country's system of distributing goods from farms and factories to consumers suffered a steady breakdown.

Soviet citizens began to give up hope that their lives would ever improve or that socialism could ever provide them with the prosperous future promised by Marx and Lenin. The result was growing cynicism and despair.

In 1980 Polish workers founded the first independent labor union under a Communist government. "Solidarity," which opposed Poland's Communist government, was a direct threat to the Brezhnev Doctrine. In response, Brezhnev ordered Soviet tank divisions to take up positions along the Polish border. The Soviets drew up plans for an invasion. But in late 1981, the Polish leader, Wojciech Jaruselzski, declared martial law and banned Solidarity. Forced underground, Solidarity was the beginning of a popular movement against Soviet rule that would spread throughout eastern Europe in the 1980s. Brezhnev did not respond to this cynicism, for he preferred to follow the Communist party's established policies. He had little imagination and was unable to create an answer to the growing restlessness among people living under Communist rule.

Brezhnev had been under quiet attack in the Politburo as other members, noticing his poor health, maneuvered to gain an advantage after his death. On November 10, 1982, Brezhnev died of a heart attack at the age of 75. Without a set procedure for electing a successor, Chernenko, Andropov, and others scrambled to gain allies who would vote them into the job. Meanwhile, the country was slipping into economic decline, and the prospects for change were dim. Every Politburo member except one was at least 70 years old. The exception was 51-year-old Mikhail Gorbachev, a little-known agricultural expert from the Stavropol territory in the southern USSR.

5

Yuri Andropov
and
Konstantin Chernenko

*L*eonid Brezhnev and the Communist party had changed little in the 1970s. Brezhnev, enjoying the privileges of high office, was not interested in making changes in a system that had served him well. Although the Soviet economy was weakening, most of those privileged in the nomenklatura—members of the Soviet bureaucracy—sought only to maintain their power and prosperity. Others, however, saw economic trouble as a threat to their jobs and their country. They knew that

By the early 1980s, Yuri Andropov knew that changes were necessary to reverse the economic decline of the Soviet Union.

changes were necessary. They also knew that reforming the entire system would be a difficult—and dangerous—task. One of these reformers was Brezhnev's successor, Yuri Andropov.

Andropov was born in 1914 in the Stavropol territory of southern Russia. He grew up in the town of Nagutskaya, where his father was a railroad station-master and his mother a piano teacher. Andropov's parents died while he was still young. He left home in the early 1930s and found work as an assistant to a movie projectionist. He later traveled to the Volga River region, where he worked on riverboats as a porter and as a sailor.

In 1932 Andropov entered the Ribinsk Water Transport Technicum, a school on the Volga River that educated students in navigation and seamanship. Although he loved the river and wanted to work as a boat captain, Andropov also had a talent for politics. He joined the Komsomol, a Communist union of young people, in the Ribinsk school and quickly became its leader.

In 1936, the year of his graduation, Andropov found work at a local shipyard, where he again became a Komsomol leader. Local Party officials saw promise in the young worker, and in 1937, they sent him to the Yaroslav region, where he joined a regional Komsomol committee. In 1939 he became a Komsomol first secretary and also joined the Communist party.

In 1940 the Party transferred Andropov to Karelia, a region of northwestern Russia along the border with Finland. Both Finnish and Russian people lived in Karelia, and tensions between the two groups were high. After a short but bloody war between the Soviet Union and Finland in 1939-40, Josef Stalin annexed part of Finland to Karelia. But in the summer of 1941, while Germany launched its invasion of the Soviet Union, the Finnish army again seized Karelia.

During the rest of the war, Andropov organized Soviet guerrilla fighters in the region and took part in building an important railroad line. After the war, Andropov imposed Soviet control over the region's cities and people. The army and police brutally stopped resistance to Stalin's rule in the northern territory. In 1947 the government promoted Andropov to a powerful position within the Karelian Communist party. He soon gained a valuable ally in Otto Kuusinen, the Communist leader in the Karelia region. In 1951 Kuusinen brought Andropov to Moscow to join the Central Committee bureaucracy.

Three years later Andropov became an ambassador in the Soviet Foreign Ministry. His assignment was Hungary, a nation that Soviet troops had occupied after World War II. His experience in Karelia proved useful in Hungary, where open revolt against local Communist leaders erupted in 1956. As ambassador to Hungary, Andropov played an important role in the Soviet invasion, which put a violent end to the revolt against the country's Communist rulers.

His superiors in Moscow praised Andropov's good work in Hungary and brought him back to the capital in 1957. In 1961 Andropov became a voting member of the Central Committee. His specialty was foreign affairs, especially relations with the socialist countries under Soviet control in eastern Europe. In 1964 Communist leaders in Moscow gave him the honor of delivering a speech to commemorate Lenin's birthday.

Moving up the ranks, Andropov became chairman of the KGB, the Soviet Union's vast state police and espionage agency. By the time of Andropov's 1967 appointment, the KGB had control over a huge network of border guards, spies, internal police, and prisons. But the KGB also employed computer specialists, data analysts, engineers, and radio specialists. It was one of the most powerful institutions in the Soviet Union and enjoyed some independence from the rest of the government.

Andropov overhauled the KGB by bringing in younger, better-educated employees. A strong-willed manager, he punished corruption and incompetence and forced out older KGB officials left from Stalin's time. His actions gained him the loyalty of this huge organization, a loyalty that would smooth his path to the leadership of the Soviet Union.

In the early 1980s, as Leonid Brezhnev's health began to fail, Andropov campaigned for the job of general secretary. In the spring of 1982, he became a member of the Secretariat of the Central Committee. As a member of both the Politburo and the Secretariat, Andropov was able to leave the KGB and gain allies in the highest levels of the Soviet government. His new political appointments paid off quickly. Two days after Brezhnev died on November 10, 1982, the Central Committee elected Andropov general secretary of the Communist party.

After presiding over Brezhnev's funeral, the new leader immediately began a drive to revitalize the Soviet bureaucracy. He had corrupt officials arrested. He forced older officials to retire and replaced them with younger men. One of these, Mikhail Gorbachev, gradually emerged as one of Andropov's most important political allies.

Andropov made visits to Soviet factories and gave frequent speeches against laziness and the lack of discipline among industrial workers. To increase the amount of goods produced, the government organized competitive teams of workers in several plants. The pay for each team depended on the quantity and quality of their work. The government severely punished workers for laziness and drunkenness. Andropov also announced plans to give local factory managers more responsibility for running their businesses. By the summer of 1983, Soviet production figures were already rising.

In May 1983, Andropov (right) welcomes staunch Soviet ally Erich Honecker, leader of East Germany.

His many years at the head of the KGB strengthened Andropov's efforts at streamlining the Soviet system. The extensive KGB files, which contained information on millions of Soviet individuals, terrified corrupt officials. Andropov had access to these files, and didn't hesitate to put them to use. Nearly 20 percent of the local Party secretaries throughout the Soviet Union lost their jobs during his term.

Andropov had less success in foreign affairs. The United States was planning to place nuclear missiles in western Europe in late 1983. To fight this deployment, the media of the Soviet Union played on fears of nuclear war among the Europeans. Massive demonstrations took place in West Germany and Britain. By the fall of 1983, a war of words had broken out between the two superpowers—the USSR and the United States. Negotiations to limit nuclear arms came to a complete stop.

In September, the Soviet Union suffered a propaganda defeat when a Korean airliner was shot down by a Soviet fighter over the Sea of Japan, off the Soviet Union's Pacific coast. While Andropov and the Soviet Union came under harsh international criticism, the United States deployed its new missiles in Europe. In the fall, the Soviet Union announced plans to deploy new missiles of its own—in eastern Europe. The two countries seemed to be moving closer to a disastrous open conflict.

Many of these events happened with Andropov out

of the picture. The Soviet leader was seen less and less in public. Without his presence, the reform program lost momentum. As Andropov began to miss important official functions, rumors of his poor health went around the Soviet capital. In fact, Andropov was suffering from kidney failure. By the winter of 1983, he was living in a hospital in the Kremlin, the Soviet center of government. Although he made a great impact on many areas of the Soviet economy and on the Communist party, Andropov's poor health effectively stopped his reform program.

In January 1984, as Andropov struggled for his life, members of the Politburo met in secret to decide on his successor. Although many Politburo members sided with Mikhail Gorbachev, the election went to Konstantin Chernenko. Chernenko assumed office a few days after Andropov's death on February 10, 1984.

Politburo conservatives, who weren't ready for Andropov's changes, elected Chernenko. Many of these conservatives were men from Brezhnev's time. They had resisted Andropov's reforms, and saw the younger Mikhail Gorbachev as a threat to their jobs. A devoted Brezhnev aide, Chernenko would turn back these reforms, or at least fail to enforce them, and return the Soviet Union to Brezhnev-style management.

Chernenko grew up far from Moscow, in the small Siberian village of Bolshaya Tes, where he was born in

1911. His family was poor and, after the death of his mother, Chernenko worked for a Siberian farmer to support his brothers and sisters. At the age of 15 he joined the Komsomol. Three years later he became a director of "agitation and propaganda" for the youth organization.

The young Siberian joined the Soviet army's border guards in 1930. His unit patrolled the frontier between China and Siberia. There the unit fought smugglers and anti-Communist rebels. In the next year he joined the Communist party. After leaving the army, he continued to work for Stalin's regime as a propagandist and may have taken part in Stalin's purge of wealthy Siberian peasants.

During World War II, Chernenko supervised the relocation of factories from western Russia to Siberia. While the German forces rolled across the Ukraine and southern Russia, the Russian people dismantled many plants and moved them to the east in order to keep up the production of important weapons. After the war, Chernenko joined the Communist party in Moldavia, a small republic near the Romanian border that Stalin had forced into the Soviet Union in 1940. In Moldavia, Chernenko met the man who would bring him to the very top of the Communist party—Leonid Brezhnev.

Brezhnev, as first secretary of Moldavia, was responsible for the "Russification" of the former Romanian territory. To bring this about, he employed Chernenko as his propaganda chief. Chernenko's task was to persuade the Moldavians that their future lay with the Soviet Union. Gradually resistance to Soviet control lessened in the late 1940s and early 1950s.

Brezhnev's success in Moldavia earned him a promotion to the Politburo in the 1950s. By that time, Chernenko had proven both his loyalty to Brezhnev and his ability as a Soviet propagandist. Brezhnev brought him to Moscow and made him chief of an important Central Committee department. In 1965, after Brezhnev and his allies had forced Nikita Khrushchev to resign, Chernenko became the head of the General Department of the Central Committee.

In this job, Chernenko controlled Brezhnev's appointments and handled important classified documents. Although he was a man of only average intelligence, he had an excellent memory and served Brezhnev well as a personal secretary. In the 1970s, as Brezhnev's health began to fail, Chernenko became even closer to his chief, constantly accompanying him to important meetings and supervising his daily schedule.

Brezhnev made sure that his trusted aide earned several important new posts in the 1970s. Chernenko became a full member of the Central Committee in 1971 and joined the committee's Secretariat in 1976. In 1978 he became a full member of the Politburo. Chernenko also took part in many of the high-level meetings between the Soviet Union and the United States concerning nuclear weapons.

Although Chernenko played an important role in the Soviet government, he did not win election as general secretary after Brezhnev's death in 1982. Many powerful officials, unhappy with the inactivity and economic decline of Brezhnev's last years, favored Yuri Andropov. Although this setback seemed to put an end to Chernenko's career, he remained in several Party jobs. As Andropov's reforms began to upset the government establishment, conservatives in the Politburo turned to Chernenko as the best alternative to Mikhail Gorbachev.

The Politburo's conservative majority elected Chernenko as general secretary after Andropov's death in February 1984. Chernenko did not disappoint his supporters. He stopped Andropov's order to cut 20 percent of the bureaucracy. Thus, he allowed thousands of Party members to return to their jobs. He ordered that officials jailed for corruption during Andropov's term be released. Chernenko also forced several of Andropov's allies out of their positions in the government and in the Soviet media.

The Soviet Union in 1984 had lost a diplomatic battle with the United States over new nuclear missiles stationed in western Europe. The Soviet press loudly criticized U.S. actions in Europe, and the Soviet military

Konstantin Chernenko addresses the Soviet parliament in April 1984.

feared the "Star Wars" space-defense system the United States was developing. Because the United States had boycotted the Olympic Games in Moscow in 1980, the Soviet Union announced it would not compete in the Summer Olympic Games in Los Angeles in 1984.

Chernenko was a practical man who feared the consequences of these rising tensions with the United States. Despite the Soviet government's frequent hostile announcements in the official Party newspapers, Chernenko sought to improve relations with the United States and with western Europe. In the spring of 1984, he proposed a new round of negotiations on the "Star Wars" system. Eventually the United States agreed, but only if the Soviet Union would also negotiate the reduction of intercontinental nuclear missiles that the two countries were aiming at each other.

In the winter of 1984, diplomats from both sides agreed to meet in Geneva, Switzerland. The confrontation between the two superpowers had come to an end, and a new round of negotiations was beginning. Although U.S. missiles in Europe would stay in place, the United States had agreed to negotiate on space defenses. Eventually, in the late 1980s, these negotiations would result in a treaty to share "Star Wars" technology and to reduce the amount of nuclear armaments on both sides.

Chernenko had achieved a diplomatic breakthrough, but he did not remain in office long enough to see the negotiations through. The oldest man ever to become general secretary, he suffered from emphysema and a weak heart, and the strain of public office brought on a serious illness. He missed several important Party ceremonies in early 1985. The members of the Politburo had been expecting Chernenko's death for some time and had already met in secret to nominate his successor. After Chernenko died on March 10, 1985, Mikhail Gorbachev quickly moved into the job as general secretary. The future that Politburo conservatives had feared was close at hand.

Mikhail Gorbachev needed all of the negotiating skills at his disposal to steer a middle course between conservative hardliners and liberal reformers in the Soviet government and Communist party.

6
Mikhail Gorbachev

Konstantin Chernenko's death in March 1985 left the Soviet Union at a crossroads. The nation had lost three leaders during the past 30 months. After a short period of improvement under Yuri Andropov, the economy was again stagnant. The aging members of the Politburo were offering no new ideas, and the huge Communist party bureaucracy was fighting reforms. Life was growing more difficult for Soviet workers. Many of them, old enough to remember Stalin, looked back on the dictator's reign as a time of progress, stability, and hope for a better future. Thirty years after Stalin, their leaders were not even offering hope.

Nikita Khrushchev, the last Soviet leader to attempt

reforms in the Communist party, had lost his job as general secretary 20 years before. Although he had made important changes, Khrushchev remained dedicated to socialism—the idea that government could manage the economy and provide for all. He was certain that modernizing the Soviet system would bring his country both prosperity and global power. For his efforts, Khrushchev was pushed out of the leadership by his rivals. Under his successors, the country grew poorer, and its people became discouraged.

Like Khrushchev, Mikhail Sergeyevich Gorbachev was raised in a small rural village. His father, Sergei Gorbachev, was a farm laborer who made his home in Privolnoye, a village in the Stavropol territory of southern Russia. Although a mild climate and rich soil made farming easier in Stavropol than in other Russian areas, the region went through its share of troubled times. In 1931, the year of Mikhail Gorbachev's birth, the peasant families of Stavropol, like peasants throughout the Soviet Union, were going through Stalin's brutal collectivization.

This drive to force peasants onto collective farms brought resistance, but resistance brought punishment, hunger, and fear. Farmers throughout the Soviet Union were turning against each other to gain the advantage. In the mid-1930s a neighbor denounced Gorbachev's grandfather, Andrei, for hoarding grain in his home. The government arrested Andrei and sent him to a distant labor camp for several years.

Although he was still a boy, Mikhail Gorbachev would not forget the disappearance of his grandfather. Seeing his family suffer at the hands of a brutal regime—as Lenin had—would deeply affect Gorbachev's outlook in the future. He could not speak out publicly against Stalin, but he would oppose the Stalinist system during his rise to the top of the Communist party.

After World War II, Mikhail Gorbachev became an assistant to a combine operator. He learned to operate and repair many different kinds of farm machinery. For his hard work in the fields and his high marks at the local school, he won recognition and several awards from the Communist party officials in Stavropol. When he was 19, local officials recommended him for entrance to the prestigious Moscow State University.

Gorbachev arrived in the Soviet capital in 1950. As a college student, he took an interest in many different subjects, including history, literature, physics, and mathematics. However, he was both ambitious and practical. He decided to work for a degree in law, a subject that would prepare him for a political career. At the university, he also joined the Komsomol, the Communist youth group. In 1952, he became a full member of the Communist party.

A talented speaker who loved to debate, Gorbachev made a strong impression on his classmates and his teachers. He made friends easily and enjoyed talking about books, movies, and politics. He became a *komsorg*—a Komsomol organizer—for his university class. A komsorg was responsible for watching closely over other Komsomol members and for making sure of their loyalty to Josef Stalin and to the Communist party. Gorbachev and other Komsomol members always spoke in support of the government's harsh policies and strict discipline. In private, however, Gorbachev expressed secret doubts and criticism about Stalinism.

Gorbachev graduated from the university in 1955.

Gorbachev and Raisa Maximovna Titorenko—the woman he married in 1954—met during a ballroom dancing class at Moscow State University.

Although he had a chance to win a secure Party job in the capital, he decided to return to Stavropol. There he joined the local Komsomol committees. Gorbachev rose quickly within these organizations. He won promotions with his hard work and his talent for speaking, debating, and persuading. His friends and colleagues could see that Gorbachev was a natural politician.

In the late 1950s, while Gorbachev was living in Stavropol, the Communist party was shaken by Nikita Khrushchev's "secret speech" at the 20th Party Congress. The speech was read aloud at Party meetings in Stavropol and all over the Soviet Union. Gorbachev and many other young Communists greeted Khrushchev's sharp criticism of the Stalinist system—the first such criticism ever expressed in public—with enthusiasm. They believed that Khrushchev would now rescue the nation from the Stalinist system and modernize the Soviet economy.

During Khrushchev's term as general secretary, Gorbachev quickly climbed the Party ladder within his home province. In 1960 he became the Komsomol leader in Stavropol. He formed a close alliance with Fyodor Kulakov, the first secretary of the Stavropol Communist party. In 1962, Kulakov moved Gorbachev into a job in the Party's Stavropol headquarters. Kulakov saw in his young aide an energetic and loyal worker. In 1963, Kulakov put Gorbachev in charge of the Stavropol territory's collective farms.

In his first position of real responsibility, Gorbachev wasted no time in making changes. To make the territory more productive, he reorganized Stavropol's farms and distribution system. Under Gorbachev's direction, farmers were allowed to expand their private plots, on which they could grow crops for profit. To gain more practical experience in the field of agriculture, Gorbachev entered an agricultural night school in 1964. Later he gained a degree in agronomy, a branch of agriculture that deals with crop production and soil management.

While Gorbachev was changing farming in Stavropol, Nikita Khrushchev was trying to reform the Communist party. Khrushchev wanted to do two things: limit the terms of Party officials and change the rules that allowed these officials to win their jobs at each election automatically. Gorbachev supported Khrushchev's agricultural reforms, which gave farmers a chance to sell any extra crops they harvested on an open market. Although they were both making changes, Khrushchev and Gorbachev would always work within the socialist system. They both believed in the ability of the central government to manage and develop the Soviet economy.

In 1964 rival leaders forced Khrushchev out of office. These politicians saw his reforms as a threat to their authority. Local Party officials who ran factories, farms, and provincial governments also opposed

Khrushchev. They had no interest in changing a system that was providing them with secure jobs and a good living. Instead, they blocked the changes by simply going about their business in the old way.

Khrushchev's fall held an important lesson for Gorbachev: any leader who wanted to modernize the Soviet system would have to gain the support of the powerful Soviet bureaucracy. Gorbachev also learned that loyalty was necessary to rise within the system. Officials replaced or simply passed over for promotion anyone who displeased or criticized those in higher positions. After Leonid Brezhnev became general secretary, Gorbachev would rarely publicly criticize either Brezhnev or Brezhnev's policies.

In the 1960s, as the farms of Stavropol became more productive, Gorbachev won praise for his agricultural reforms. By his own hard work and innovation, Gorbachev was helping Fyodor Kulakov make his reputation as the boss of a prosperous agricultural region. Kulakov eventually gained a seat on the Central Committee of the Communist party and later was appointed to the Politburo.

In 1970, with the backing of Kulakov, the Party appointed Gorbachev first secretary of the Stavropol Communist organization. Over the next few years, he had many opportunities to meet the most powerful men in the Soviet Union, including Brezhnev, Yuri Andropov, and Konstantin Chernenko. Kulakov often brought these Soviet leaders to Stavropol, which was a popular region for official retreats and summer vacations.

While boss of Stavropol, Gorbachev made several reforms including a system of bonus payments for good crop harvests. Although some of his ideas were unsuccessful, Gorbachev's good connections in Moscow helped him to overcome any setbacks. Stavropol's harvests during the 1970s usually met the government's expectations.

Many other parts of the country, however, were not doing so well. Under Brezhnev's rule, the Soviet economy was stagnating. Consumer goods were in short supply. An illegal black market in stolen goods caused theft and bribery among managers, government officials, and workers.

Many Soviet officials were unhappy with the situation. Yuri Andropov, the head of the Soviet state police (KGB), was an energetic leader who enjoyed some independence from the Politburo. Andropov and others within the KGB saw the economic decline as a serious threat to the future of the Soviet Union. To meet the problem, they sought out younger officials who were trying new ideas. Gorbachev, who was attracting attention with his successful reforms in Stavropol, won the support and encouragement of the powerful KGB chief in the 1970s.

In 1978, after the death of Fyodor Kulakov,

Andropov arranged Gorbachev's appointment to the Secretariat of the Central Committee. Even for a talented and well-connected Party member, this was a surprising promotion. Most members of the Secretariat had to serve long terms as ordinary Central Committee members before they could hope for further promotion.

The youngest member of the Soviet leadership, Gorbachev was now in charge of agriculture for the entire country. He immediately put more reforms to work. He transferred control of farming from Moscow to local authorities; he awarded bonuses to farm laborers for high crop production; finally, he allowed collective farms to sell some of their harvests on the open market instead of to the state.

However, despite Gorbachev's efforts, farm production declined during the next few years. The government made little investment in new machinery and the transportation system continued to deteriorate. Nevertheless, the young agriculture secretary weathered the crisis and kept Andropov's confidence. In 1980 Gorbachev became the youngest full member of the Politburo.

In 1982, after Brezhnev's death, Soviet leaders elected Andropov as general secretary. The new leader openly criticized Brezhnev's inactivity and called for reforms. He replaced local Party bosses with younger men and reduced the huge staffs of local Party committees. Within a few months, however, Andropov's health began to fail. Realizing that his time was limited, he brought Mikhail Gorbachev into his inner circle of advisors in an attempt to prepare the younger man for the leadership of the Soviet Union.

Despite Andropov's attempt to make Gorbachev his heir, a majority of Politburo members considered Gorbachev too inexperienced or too liberal for the top job. Instead, they elected Konstantin Chernenko, a close aide to Leonid Brezhnev, as general secretary after Andropov's death in February 1984.

The conservative Chernenko slowed Andropov's reforms and promised no further actions that might upset the Party bureaucracy. Most of the older Politburo members formed a closely knit group around Chernenko. Suspicious of the younger and more energetic Gorbachev, these men defended the traditional central planning and management of the Soviet economy.

The result of their rigidity was continued economic decline. Many Communist officials now openly accepted bribes, and sold stolen goods on the illegal black market. Shortages of food and consumer goods worsened. A cloud of distrust and pessimism descended over the nation. With an old Brezhnev crony in power, the Soviet people despaired of ever seeing any change for the better.

Despite Chernenko's election, Mikhail Gorbachev had become the second secretary and continued his efforts to create a "market socialism." He favored the creation of a free market, supervised and planned by the central government. He traveled to Britain and other European countries, and made a strong impression on the Western media as a dynamic and imaginative politician. Gorbachev also gained favor among a few conservative members of the Politburo. As Chernenko's health began to fail, Gorbachev emerged as a strong candidate to succeed Chernenko as general secretary.

Chernenko's term was the shortest in Soviet history. Within a year of taking power, he was hospitalized and, in March 1985, he died. Members of the Politburo scrambled to form alliances and elect the next general secretary. Although many thought that Gorbachev was the best candidate, his election as general secretary was not assured. Several conservatives still opposed him but they were unable to put forward a stronger candidate. At a meeting of the Central Committee, Andrei Gromyko, the Soviet Union's foreign minister, threw his support to Gorbachev, commenting, "This man has a nice smile, comrades, but he's got iron teeth!" After Gromyko reassured conservative members of the Central Committee, they elected Gorbachev as general secretary on March 11, 1985.

In April, Gorbachev appointed several of his allies to the Politburo. He arranged the election of young reformers to the Central Committee. The Party's official newspapers denounced corrupt officials who were then forced

As Stalin's ambassador to the United States, the United Nations, and Great Britain, Andrei Gromyko had strong conservative credentials. His support was crucial to Gorbachev's election as general secretary.

to retire. Moreover, Gorbachev shifted Brezhnev's colleagues in the government to insignificant jobs.

Gorbachev was certain that by carefully explaining his plans, he could persuade suspicious Soviet bureaucrats to go along with him. "There is no turning back, comrades," he announced during a speech early in his term. "Those who cannot accept reforms must simply get out of the way."

The new general secretary acted with haste. Soviet industry was suffering from a lack of modern equipment, poor planning and distribution, and sheer laziness on the part of workers, supervisors, and managers. To fight the system's inertia, Gorbachev proposed that factory managers award bonuses to workers for the quantity and the quality of the goods they produced. State-owned factories would begin competing with each other by selling their goods at free prices. Local managers would decide how much of their product to make, and where and how to sell it. Eventually, all prices would be set by supply and demand—not by the state. Gorbachev's plan for updating the Soviet economy was called *perestroika* (restructuring).

Gorbachev and his followers also had to solve serious social problems. Alcoholism was perhaps the worst of these. Many Soviet people drank to relieve boredom, stress, and a sense of hopelessness. Factory workers came to work drunk. Alcoholism was hurting productivity and causing crime and disease. By sharply raising the price of vodka (the most popular alcohol in the Soviet Union), by limiting the hours it could be sold in stores, and by setting severe punishments for on-the-job drunkenness, Gorbachev attacked the problem with effective but unpopular measures.

Early in his term, Gorbachev realized that he would need strong allies in order to make perestroika succeed. In July 1985, he named Eduard Shevardnadze, the Party boss of the Georgian republic, as the Soviet foreign minister. Although the appointment of a non-Russian to this post came as a surprise, Gorbachev had his way.

Other appointments, however, did not come so easily. Gorbachev also attempted to replace Viktor Grishin,

Foreign Minister Eduard Shevardnadze became Gorbachev's closest advisor, warning him of his enemies within Soviet ruling circles.

the corrupt mayor of Moscow. But Grishin was a powerful man within the Communist party and had many supporters. He had nearly succeeded Chernenko as general secretary in March 1985. Only after a long and passionate speech in front of the Central Committee did Gorbachev succeed in appointing Grishin's replacement—Boris Yeltsin.

A popular reformer from the city of Sverdlovsk, east of the Ural Mountains, Yeltsin, a strong critic of communism's problems, drew friendly crowds at his many public appearances. Yeltsin insisted that the Soviet

140

economy and political system needed a complete over-haul. He pushed Gorbachev to institute nationwide, free elections and a completely open-market economy.

To gather public support for his ideas, Gorbachev announced a new policy of *glasnost* (openness). Glasnost meant that writers were now free to criticize both the past mistakes and the present problems of the Soviet system. Glasnost freed newspapers, books, magazines, and television of most government censorship. Under glasnost, the mass media were supposed to expose cor-ruption, bribery, theft, and incompetence among gov-ernment officials. This would then force them to mend their ways or resign their jobs.

However, having lived through decades of restric-

Once a high-ranking member of the Communist party, Boris Yeltsin emerged as the leading voice for democratic change in the USSR.

tions, writers were unsure of exactly what would now be allowed. Some leaders in eastern Europe, trained to follow the Soviet Union's lead, did ease control of newspapers. Others, fearful of public criticism, kept a tight grip on public speaking and writing. Thus, glasnost caused both excitement and confusion in the Soviet Union and in eastern Europe, where unpopular Communist regimes were kept in place by the threat of Soviet invasion. Glasnost also was a risk to Gorbachev, who had made his own reform program—with all its possible mistakes and difficulties—open to attack.

Gorbachev and the younger men he appointed made up only a small group within the huge Soviet bureaucracy, which employed millions of people. Gorbachev's reforms, which opened key positions to public election, posed a threat to many powerful officials. For this reason, many in the Communist party resisted him. By the 27th Party Congress in early 1986, opposition to Gorbachev was growing. Yegor Ligachev, a Politburo official from Siberia, was speaking out in praise of Stalin and Brezhnev, and against many of Gorbachev's reforms.

Gorbachev and glasnost were put to the test on April 26, 1986, when an explosion destroyed a nuclear power plant at Chernobyl in Ukraine. The disaster released a cloud of radioactivity that eventually reached northern and central Europe. However, the government did not tell the public about the accident for several days. With

142

Secretary of the Communist party Central Committee, Yegor Ligachev helped to organize opposition to Gorbachev among Soviet hardliners.

thousands of lives in danger, the Soviet government covered up the bad news. The incident became an embarrassment for Gorbachev who seemed to have little control of events or of his own government. Glasnost, to many, seemed to be an empty promise.

In 1987 the Central Committee approved many of Gorbachev's proposed economic reforms. Now, Soviet firms could operate without interference from the government's planning bureaus. Under Gorbachev's

A Soviet helicopter hovers over the damaged nuclear reactor at Chernobyl.

reforms, companies were supposed to be entirely free of central planning by 1991. Unprofitable companies would be closed down. Prices for all goods—food, machinery, appliances, and clothing—would be set by producers, wholesalers, and shops.

Gorbachev gave perestroika two years to succeed in changing the Soviet economy. He assumed that, with his own persuasion and with glasnost, Soviet citizens would eventually support his program.

Many workers, however, did not accept perestroika. They preferred stability to freedom. Perestroika threatened to end socialism's benefits—free education, free medical care, low-cost housing, guaranteed employment—while replacing them with nothing but promises of a better future. For many workers, wages began to decline. Food shortages continued. In the summer of 1988, one year after perestroika was approved by the Central Committee, the first strikes in protest over the new policy took place.

Despite criticism, Gorbachev pressed on. He knew that once central planning was lessened, turning back the Soviet economy would be impossible. A free market was inevitable—and the Soviet Union could not avoid the problems of making the transition.

An important way to ease the pressure on the economy was to reduce the Soviet Union's enormous defense budget. To achieve this, Gorbachev decided to negotiate with the United States on the two countries'

At the 1985 summit in Geneva, Soviet Foreign Minister Eduard Shevardnadze and U.S. Secretary of State George Shultz sign an agreement on Soviet-American cultural exchanges, as Soviet General Secretary Mikhail Gorbachev and U.S. President Ronald Reagan look on.

arsenals, or storehouses, of nuclear weapons. He agreed to several meetings with Ronald Reagan, who had been elected president of the United States in 1980. A tough critic of the Soviet Union, Reagan challenged the policy of détente that, during Brezhnev's term, had eased tensions between the Soviet Union and the West.

In the early 1980s, Reagan announced plans for the Strategic Defense Initiative (SDI), a new space-based defense system that would put the Soviet Union behind in the arms race. In 1985 Gorbachev met with Reagan in Geneva, Switzerland. Gorbachev's goals were simple:

146

to improve relations with the West, to stop SDI, and to limit the number of nuclear weapons so that the Soviet Union could save money and rebuild its economy. Although the Geneva meeting was not a success, Gorbachev made a favorable impression on Reagan and on Western newspaper reporters. From that point on, U.S. and European newspapers closely followed his actions as general secretary.

Gorbachev's negotiations with the United States were an important part of a plan to reform the Soviet military. But the Soviet armed forces were a powerful obstacle. Soviet generals opposed negotiations with the United States, and a huge, state-owned weapons industry opposed any limit on defense spending.

To challenge the military, Gorbachev needed an excuse—which he received on May 28, 1987, when Matthias Rust, a German teenager, flew a small private plane through Soviet air defenses and landed in the center of Moscow. After this embarrassing incident, the Soviet military came under sharp criticism in the press. The Soviet leadership fired air force leaders. Gorbachev also forced military officials opposed to him out of their jobs.

In the next summer, Gorbachev announced that the Communist governments in eastern Europe would have to stand on their own. No longer would Soviet tanks and troops support unpopular socialist leaders or invade eastern European countries that were in revolt. With the people of eastern Europe openly calling for democratic elections, Gorbachev's decision meant the swift end of the "Brezhnev Doctrine" and of Soviet control of the region. Within six months, Communist leaders had fallen from power in East Germany, Hungary, Czechoslovakia, Bulgaria, Romania, and Poland. Gorbachev also announced plans to withdraw Soviet forces from Afghanistan, where a small army of Afghan anti-Communist guerrillas had fought the Red Army to a stalemate.

Although Gorbachev was gaining attention and approval in the West for his actions, many in the Soviet Union openly challenged perestroika in 1987. In his speeches and writings, Yegor Ligachev claimed that perestroika threatened the end of socialism. Viktor Chebrikov, the chief of the KGB, supported Ligachev. If these two men gathered enough allies, they could put a swift end to Gorbachev's reforms, just as Suslov and Brezhnev had put an end to Khrushchev's reforms 25 years before.

Gorbachev still had powerful supporters, one of the most popular being Boris Yeltsin. In a surprise speech to the Central Committee in October 1987, Yeltsin scolded Ligachev and demanded reforms even more radical than Gorbachev had proposed. His speech shocked the Central Committee and brought Gorbachev under fire from conservative Party members. Despite his popularity among the residents of

Moscow, Yeltsin was forced to resign his post. Gorbachev could not—or would not—protect him.

In the spring of 1988, Gorbachev realized that perestroika would succeed only with a complete overhaul of the Party bureaucracy. In June he announced sweeping changes in the Soviet government. He sought to create a new, openly elected Soviet parliament, elected local councils, and an executive presidency that would be limited to two five-year terms. In the fall, the Central Committee voted on and passed these reforms. This was the beginning of the end of the Party's hold on power.

Another conservative critic of Gorbachev, KGB chairman Viktor Chebrikov built his political career as a loyal follower of Leonid Brezhnev.

By 1991, despite all of Gorbachev's many efforts to ensure its success, perestroika was widely seen as a failure. Shortages and corruption persisted. Russian businesses had difficulty competing in an open market, and many were failing. Gorbachev even found himself opposed by Boris Yeltsin, who was now criticizing perestroika for not moving quickly toward a complete market economy.

In addition, glasnost was leading to growing demands for independence among the Soviet republics, many of which had been forced into the Soviet Union. Lithuania, in the Baltic region, declared its independence. Open elections took place in Estonia and Latvia, where the Communist candidates were defeated. These events caused great alarm among conservative Communist officials. Ligachev and others spoke openly of turning back perestroika and putting an end to glasnost. Fearing a conservative coup against Gorbachev, Eduard Shevardnadze shocked the country by quitting his post as foreign minister. Shevardnadze warned at an open meeting of the Central Committee that dictatorship was now threatening the Soviet Union.

To preserve the union, Gorbachev proposed a treaty in the summer of 1991 that would allow the Soviet republics a greater degree of self-government. On August 19, the day before the treaty was to be signed, several Politburo members and military leaders—including Ligachev—attempted to seize power illegally.

Uniformed officials confined Gorbachev at his vacation home. To back up their actions, the coup leaders ordered tanks into the streets of Moscow.

Boris Yeltsin, who had been elected president of Russia after quitting the Communist party, rallied support in front of the Russian parliament building in Moscow. Thousands of residents took to the streets, building barricades and blocking tanks and trucks. After a few days, the coup collapsed and Gorbachev was released.

The failed overthrow showed that the Communist party was now completely disorganized and incapable of controlling the Soviet Union. Within a week, several republics declared their independence. Gorbachev could do nothing to stop them. In December 1991, Ukrainians voted in favor of independence. Yeltsin and the leaders of Byelorussia and Ukraine then announced a new Commonwealth of Independent States, with its capital in the city of Minsk. Eight other republics quickly joined the Commonwealth. Yeltsin closed the Communist party's Moscow headquarters and the power of the Soviet central government quickly melted away.

On December 25, Gorbachev resigned his office. He had fought the break up of the Soviet Union until, with the fall of the Communist party, the independence of the fifteen republics that had made up the Soviet Union became inevitable. Gorbachev still insisted that the former Soviet republics stood a better chance of

The Soviet military answer their leaders' August 1991 call to the streets of Moscow, but do not fire on their countrymen.

With Gorbachev detained, Boris Yeltsin leads mass demonstrations against the coup leaders, whom the public fear could return the country to Stalinism.

152

After the coup attempt failed, a shaken Mikhail Gorbachev steps off the airplane that returned him, his wife, Raisa, granddaughter Ksenia, and other family members to Moscow on August 22, 1991. Four months later, a frustrated Gorbachev would resign from office.

surviving in a strong, centrally controlled union. As a Soviet leader who grew up in an era of absolute central authority, he could not agree to the result of his own economic and political reforms—democracy and the independence of the Soviet republics. Time will tell whether the leaders of the new Commonwealth of Independent States have found a better way.

Bibliography

Conquest, Robert. *V.I. Lenin.* New York: Viking Press, 1972.

Dallin, Alexander and Rice, Condoleezza, eds. *The Gorbachev Era.* Stanford, CA: Stanford Alumni Association, 1986.

Doder, Dusko. *Gorbachev: Heretic in the Kremlin.* New York: Viking Press, 1990.

——————————. *Shadows and Whispers: Power Politics Inside the Kremlin from Brezhnev to Gorbachev.* New York: Random House, 1986.

Hoobler, Dorothy and Thomas. *Joseph Stalin.* New York: Chelsea House Publishers, 1987.

Khrushchev, Nikita. *Khrushchev Remembers.* Translated by Strobe Talbott. Boston: Little, Brown, 1970.

Kochan, Lionel. *Lenin.* Wayland History Makers. London: Wayland Publishers, 1974.

Kort, Michael. *Nikita Khrushchev.* New York: Franklin Watts, 1989.

Navazelskis, Ina L. *Leonid Brezhnev.* New York: Chelsea House, 1988.

Reed, John. *Ten Days that Shook the World.* New York: The Modern Library, 1935.

Topalian, Elyse. *V.I. Lenin.* New York: Franklin Watts, 1983.

Volgokonov, Dimitri. *Stalin: Triumph and Tragedy.* Translated by Harold Shukman. New York: Grove Weidenfeld, 1991.

Index

Afghanistan, 109-110, 148
Africa, 14, 103
agriculture, 41, 57, 91; effect on, of collectivization, 57-58, 95, 128, 135; reforms of, under Gorbachev, 131, 132, 133, 135; reforms of, under Khrushchev, 81, 82, 84-87, 101, 132
Akselrod, P.B., 27
alcoholism in Soviet Union, 139
Alexander II (Russian tsar), 19, 20
Alexandra (Russian tsarina), 32
Andropov, Yuri, 15, 83, 103, 105, 112; death of, 120; early years of, 114-115; as ambassador, 116; as head of KGB, 105, 116, 117, 134; as leader of the Soviet Union, 117-120, 135-136; as member of Communist party, 115-116, 117; reforms of, 117-120, 135-136
Arsenichov Metallurgical Institute, 96-97
Asia, 14, 103

Baltic states, 61
Beria, Lavrenty, 80-81
Berlin, 65, 104
Bolsheviks, 28, 29, 30, 32, 34, 42, 45, 49, 52, 71-72; role of, in revolution, 35, 36, 38, 39, 40, 41
Brest-Litovsk, Treaty of, 40
Brezhnev, Leonid Ilyich, 14-15, 92; death of, 112; early years of, 93-94; education of, 94-95; as head of space program, 103; and Hungarian revolt, 102-103; as leader of Soviet Union, 104-112, 149; loyalty of, to Stalin, 96, 100; as member of Communist party,

96, 97, 100, 101, 104; policy of, toward dissidents, 105-106; relation of, to Khrushchev, 97, 100-101, 102-103, 104; and Strategic Arms Limitation Talks (SALT), 108-110; work of, in collectivization, 95-96, 97; during World War II, 98-99
Brezhnev Doctrine, 106, 107, 111, 148
Bulganin, Nikolai, 82, 83, 84
Bulgaria, 65, 66, 148
bureaucracy of Communist party, 13-15, 92, 96, 105, 113, 123; origins of, 12; attempted reforms of, 14, 105, 111, 117, 127, 132-133, 135-136, 138, 142, 149
Byelorussia, 42, 95, 96, 151

capitalism, 9-10
Carter, Jimmy, 109, 110
Castro, Fidel, 88
Central Committee, 40, 55, 76, 84, 100, 116, 117, 133, 137, 143, 148-149; role of, in Communist party, 53, 91, 122, 135
Chebrikov, Viktor, 148-149
Cheka, 39
Chernenko, Konstantin, 15, 100, 105, 112, 124; conservative policies of, 120, 123, 136; death of, 125, 127, 137; early years of, 120-121; as leader of Soviet Union, 123-125; as member of Communist party, 121, 122; relation of, with Brezhnev, 120, 121-123, 136
Chernobyl, explosion in nuclear power plant at, 142-144
Chernyshevsky, Nikolai, 24
China, 88
Churchill, Winston, 64

civil war (1918-1921), 11, 41,
42, 53, 71-72, 95
Cold War, 65, 103
collectivization, 57-58, 95-96,
97, 100, 128, 135
Cominform, 66
Commonwealth of Independent
States, 151, 153
communism, 10, 11, 40
Communist Manifesto, 70
Communist party, 11, 12, 43;
under Brezhnev, 104, 105,
109, 111; bureaucracy of, 12,
13, 14, 16, 67, 92, 96, 105,
113, 117, 127, 133, 137, 142,
149; dissolution of, in 1991,
151; under Gorbachev, 16,
138, 142-143, 151; under
Khrushchev, 13-14, 80, 83,
84, 91, 92; members, privileges of, 13-14, 104, 105;
reforms in, 83, 91, 102, 103,
105, 111, 114, 117, 127, 128,
132; role of, in Soviet government, 12, 13, 14, 43, 84,
97, 100-101; under Stalin, 13,
53-54
Congress of People's Deputies,
15
Council of People's
Commissars, 38
Cuba, 88-90, 104
Cuban missile crisis, 89, 90, 104
Czechoslovakia, 65, 98, 99, 148;
invasion of, by Soviet troops,
107

democracy in Soviet Union, 15,
24, 30, 153
"destalinization," 83, 85-86, 92
détente, 107-108, 109, 146
dictatorship of proletariat, 26
dissidents, 105-106, 109
Dnepropetrovsk (Ukraine), 97,
98
"doctors' plot," 67
Donbass region (Ukraine), 70,
71
Dubcek, Alexander, 107
Duma, 29, 32, 36
Dzhugashvili, Iosif
Vissarionovich. See Stalin,
Josef
Dzhugashvili, Vissarion, 46

eastern Europe, 102-103, 106,
111; move of, toward democ-
racy in 1980s, 142, 147; occu-
pied by Soviets at end of
World War II, 65, 66, 98, 99
East Germany, 65, 118, 148
Engels, Friedrich, 70
Estonia, 61, 150

famine: in Soviet Union during
1920s, 57; in Ukraine, 78
Finland, 34, 36, 50, 53, 109, 115
Five Year Plan, 57
Ford, Gerald, 108

general secretary of Communist
party, 12, 13; Andropov as,
117, 135; Chernenko as, 123,
136; Gorbachev as, 125, 138,
140; Khrushchev as, 13, 84,
101, 131; Stalin as, 13, 53, 55
Geladze, Katerina, 46
Georgia, 45-46, 47
Germany: under Hitler, 61, 77;
role of, in Russian revolution,
33-34, 35; war of, with Russia
(1914-1918), 31, 33, 35, 39-
40, 71; war of, with Soviet
Union in 1940s (World War
II), 13, 61, 62, 63, 64, 65, 77-
78, 98
Gierek, Edward, 94
glasnost, 141-142, 145, 150,
Gorbachev, Andrei, 128-129
Gorbachev, Mikhail
Sergeyevich, 15, 86, 92, 112,
120, 126, 140; as ally of
Andropov, 117-118, 134-135;
attempted coup against, 16,
151-152; early years of, 128-

129; family, 153; and glasnost, 141-142, 143, 150; as
member of Communist party,
129, 131, 133, 136-137;
negotiations of, with United
States, 145-146; opposition
of, to Stalinism, 129, 130,
131; and perestroika, 139,
145, 148; personality of, 129-
130, 131; reforms under, 16,
132, 133, 134, 138, 142, 149,
153; relation of, to Brezhnev,
133; resignation of, 16-17,
153; work of, in Stavropol,
129, 131-132, 133-134
Gorbachev, Raisa, 130, 153
Gorbachev, Sergei, 128
Gori, 45-47
Gorki, Maxim, 47
Grishin, Viktor, 139-140
Gromyko, Andrei, 137, 138

Helsinki accords, 109
Hitler, Adolf, 61, 63, 77
Honecker, Erich, 118
Hugo, Victor, 47
Hungary, 65, 148; revolt of,
against Soviet control, 83,
102-103, 116
hydrogen bomb, Soviet, 106

industrialization: in Russian
Empire, 20, 30, 93, 98; under
Stalin, 13, 57, 58, 61, 67, 98
Iowa, 85
Iskra, 26-28

Japan, war of, with Russian
Empire, 28-29
Jaruselzski, Wojciech, 111

Kaganovich, Lazar, 75
Kalinovka, 69, 70, 72
Kamenev, Lev, 54, 55, 59
Kamenskoye, 93, 95, 96, 97
Kaplan, Fanny, 41
Karelia, 115, 116
Kazakhstan, 87, 101

Kazan, University of, 23
Kennedy, John, 89, 90
Kerensky, Alexander, 35, 36, 38
KGB, 105, 116, 148; Andropov
as chairman of, 116-117, 119,
134
Khrushchev, Nikita
Sergeyevich: activities of, in
Ukraine, 74-75, 76, 77, 78,
79, 97; attack of, on Stalin,
83, 86, 92, 102, 131; as commissar, 72, 73, 75; and Cuban
missile crisis, 89, 90; death of,
92; early years of, 69-70; as
leader of Soviet Union, 84,
86, 101; as member of
Bolshevik party, 72, 73-74;
position of, in Communist
party, 73-76; reforms under,
13, 14, 83, 84-85, 86-87, 89,
91, 92, 105, 127-128, 132;
relation of, to Stalin, 74, 75,
76, 78, 79; resignation of, 91-
92, 104; rivalry of, with
Malenkov, 79, 80, 81-82, 83,
100, 101; role of, during revolution, 71, 72; "secret
speech" of, 82-83, 102, 131;
work of, in Ukrainian mines,
70, 71, 73; visit of, to United
States, 84; during World
War II, 77, 78, 79
Khrushchev, Sergei, 69-70
Kissinger, Henry, 108
Komsomol, 95, 97, 115, 121,
129, 130, 131
komsorg, 130
Korean airliner shot down, 119
Kornilov, Lvar Georgyevich, 36
Kosygin, Aleksy, 92, 94
Kruspskaya, Nadezhda, 18, 25,
26, 27
Kulakov, Fyodor, 131, 133-134
kulaks, 57-58
Kuusinen, Otto, 116

Latvia, 61, 150
Lenin, Vladimir, 10, 11, 18, 22,

51; attempt on life of, 41; birth of, 20; death of, 11, 12, 43-44; education of, 23-24; exile of, in Siberia, 26; family of, 21-23; as head of Soviet government, 39, 40-42, 43; and *Iskra*, 26-28; as leader of Bolshevik party, 28, 29, 30, 34, 35, 36, 45, 52-53, 93; opposition of, to war with Germany, 31; policies of 42-43; relationship of, to Stalin, 51, 54, 55; tomb of, 44, 94; will of, 54, 55

Leninism, 28

Ligachev, Yegor, 142, 143, 148, 150

Lithuania, 16, 61, 150

Malenkov, Georgy, 79, 80, 81, 82, 83-84, 100, 101

Mao Tse-tung, 88

"market socialism," 137, 145

Martov, Y.O., 27

Marx, Karl, 6, 9, 21, 70; economic theory of, 10, 13-15, 21, 23, 30, 44, 48

Marxists in Russia, 10, 21, 23, 25-26, 45, 48

Mensheviks, 28, 29, 34, 41, 49

Mercader, Ramón, 60

Moldavia, 100, 121-122

Molotov, Vyacheslav, 80, 83-84, 99

Moscow, 9, 17, 140; attacked by Germans (1942), 63; rioting in, 29; Soviet capital moved to, 40

Moscow Agricultural Academy, 96

Moscow Party Committee, 76

Moscow State University, 129, 130

New Economic Policy (NEP), 41-42

Nicholas II (Russian tsar), 29, 30, 31, 32, 33, 40; abdication of, 32, 34, 52; death of, 33

Nixon, Richard, 108

NKVD (secret police under Stalin), 59, 60

nomenklatura system, 105, 111, 113

nuclear weapons, 88, 89, 103, 106, 108, 119, 123; negotiations on, 119, 123, 125, 147

Okhrana, 48

Olympic Games, boycotts of: 1980, 109; 1984, 124

Omsk, 42

perestroika, 139, 145, 148-149, 150

Petrograd: seizure of, by Bolsheviks, 38, 71; soviet, 32, 36, 38; strikes in, 32, 71. *See also* St. Petersburg

Plekhanov, Georgy, 25, 27

Poland, 61, 65, 77, 83, 148; Solidarity labor union formed in, 111

Politburo, 56, 101, 112, 120, 122, 123, 135, 137; changes in name of, 101, 105; role of, 55, 76

Potresov, A.P., 27

Potsdam Conference, 64, 99

Pravda, 30, 52, 53

Presidium, 91, 101, 104, 105

provisional government, 32, 33-34, 39; fall of, 38, 53; opposition to, 35, 36, 52, 53

purges under Stalin, 43, 56, 59-60, 67, 76, 79-80, 96

quotas, production, 58, 67, 107

Red Army, 60, 61, 63, 65, 77, 78, 98, 148

Red Guards, 36, 37, 39, 53, 71, 72

Red Square, 37, 94

Reagan, Ronald, 146-147

republics, Soviet, 42; indepen-

dence of, 16-17, 150, 151, 153
revolution: predicted by Marx, 10, 23, 30, 44; in Russia, 10, 12, 23, 27, 28, 29, 32-33, 34, 44, 49, 50, 68
Ribinsk Water Transport Technicum, 115
Romania, 65, 98, 148
Romanov, 33
Roosevelt, Franklin, 64
Russia (republic), 9, 42, 151
Russian Empire, 10, 12, 42, 52; during nineteenth century, 19-21; reforms in, 29, 30, 32; revolution in, 10, 12, 27, 28, 29, 32; war of, with Japan, 28; war of, with Germany (1914-1918), 31-32
Russification, 76, 97, 100, 121
Rust, Matthias, 147
Rutchenkovo mines, 71

Sakharov, Andrei, 106
St. Petersburg, 25, 52; rioting in, 29; socialist activity in, 25, 26; soviets established in, 29; University of, 24. *See also* Petrograd
Secretariat (of Communist party), 53, 54, 117, 122, 135
"secret speech" of Khrushchev, 82-83, 102, 131
secret police, Soviet, 43, 59, 67, 81, 116-117
serfs, 19, 38, 46, 69
Shevardnadze, Eduard, 139, 140, 146; resignation of, 150
Shultz, George, 146
Simbirsk, 20, 21
Smolny Institute, 39
Social Democratic (SD) party, 26, 28, 48; divisions in, 26, 28, 49
socialism, 10, 12, 42, 106; in Africa and Asia, 14; as described by Marx, 9-10, 13, 15, 21, 23; failure of, in

Soviet Union, 13-14, 17, 68; in nineteenth-century Russia, 23, 25-26
Solidarity, 111
Solzhenitsyn, Alexander, 106
soviets, 10, 29, 32, 34, 36, 38, 40, 71
space race, 87, 103
Sputnik, 86, 87
Stalin, Josef, 51, 52: as Bolshevik, 49, 50; childhood of, 45-46; criminal acts of, 50; death of, 67, 80; as dictator, 12, 13, 56-60, 66, 68, 76, 79-80; discrediting of, 82, 83, 86, 92, 102; exile of, 49-50, 52; growing power of, in Communist party, 43, 53-54, 55, 74; and Hitler, 61, 77; industrialization under, 57-58; as member of Social Democratic party, 48, 49; personality of, 45, 46, 48, 49-50, 51-52, 56-57; purges under, 43, 56, 59-60, 67, 76, 79, 96; re-burial of, 86; role of, in revolution, 30, 50, 52, 53, 56; as seminarian, 47-48; during World War II, 61, 63, 64, 98, 99
Stalingrad, battle of, 63, 78
Stalin Industrial Academy, 75
Stalinism, 13, 92, 152
"Star Wars" defense system, 124, 125
Strategic Arms Limitation Talks (SALT), 108-110
Strategic Defense Initiative (SDI), 146, 147
Stavropol, 112, 114, 128, 131-132, 134
Suslov, Mikhail, 104

Tiflis, 47-48
Tito, Josip Broz, 65-66, 102
Transcarpathia, 98
Transcaucasian Federation, 42
Trotsky, Leon, 29, 37, 54; assas-

159

sination of, 60; as leader of
Red Guards, 36, 37, 53;
opposition of, to Stalin, 56
Truman, Harry, 64
tsars, Russian, 10, 17, 19, 20, 29,
47
Tukhachevsky, Mikhail
Nikolayevich, 60
22nd Party Congress (1961), 86
27th Party Congress (1986),
142

Ukraine, 40, 42, 57, 70, 74-75,
96; famine in, 78; indepen-
dence of, 151; invasion of, by
Germany (1918), 72; resis-
tance of, to Soviet rule, 76,
77, 78, 79; "Russification" of,
76, 97; during World War II,
77-78, 98, 99
Ukrainian Communist party,
74-75, 76, 97
Ulyanov, Alexander, 21, 22, 23,
24
Ulyanov family, 22
Ulyanov, Ilya, 21, 22
Ulyanov, Maria, 21, 22
Ulyanov, Vladimir Ilyich. *See*
Lenin, Vladimir
Union of Soviet Socialist
Republics (USSR), 11, 16, 17;
founding of, 42

United Nations, 109
United States, 10, 41, 65, 66;
and Cold War, 65, 103; and
Cuban missile crisis, 89, 104;
détente of, with Soviet
Union, 107-108; negotiations
of, with Soviet Union, 103,
107-109, 119, 123, 124, 145-
146; visit of Khrushchev to,
84

"war communism," 40
What Is to Be Done?, 24-25
White forces, 41, 42, 71-72
Winter Palace, 38, 53
World War I, 30-31, 65, 71
World War II, 61, 62, 63, 65,
66, 67, 98
"wreckers," 59

Yeltsin, Boris, 140-141, 149; rise
of, to power, 151-152
Yenukidze, Avel, 47
Yugoslavia, 65-66, 102
Yuzovka, 70, 71, 73
Yuzovka Workers Faculty, 73

Zasulich, V. I., 27
Zhukov, Georgy, 80, 81
Zinoviev, Grigory, 54, 55, 59

Photo Credits

Photographs courtesy of Library of Congress: pp. 8, 11, 20, 33,
35, 38, 44, 47, 55, 66, 80, 82, 88; Russian Embassy, Washington,
D.C.: pp. 16, 18, 22 (all), 27, 31, 37 (both), 39, 42, 51, 60, 62
(both), 63, 64 (both), 74, 81, 87, 94, 99, 102, 104, 106, 110 (bottom), 114, 118, 124, 130, 138, 140, 141, 143, 144, 146, 149, 152
(both), 153, front cover; STAR TRIBUNE/Minneapolis-St. Paul,
pp. 85, 126, back cover; John F. Kennedy Library, p. 90 (both);
Gerald R. Ford Library, p. 108; Jimmy Carter Library, p.110 (top).